CHINA IN TRANSITION

HUMAN RIGHTS IN CHINA

SELECTED EXAMINATIONS

CHINA IN TRANSITION

Additional books in this series can be found on Nova's website under the Series tab.

Additional e-books in this series can be found on Nova's website under the e-book tab.

CHINA IN TRANSITION

HUMAN RIGHTS IN CHINA

SELECTED EXAMINATIONS

KIMBERLY AUSTIN
EDITOR

nova publishers

New York

For permission to use material from this book please contact us:
Telephone 631-231-7269; Fax 631-231-8175
Web Site: http://www.novapublishers.com

NOTICE TO THE READER

The Publisher has taken reasonable care in the preparation of this book, but makes no expressed or implied warranty of any kind and assumes no responsibility for any errors or omissions. No liability is assumed for incidental or consequential damages in connection with or arising out of information contained in this book. The Publisher shall not be liable for any special, consequential, or exemplary damages resulting, in whole or in part, from the readers' use of, or reliance upon, this material. Any parts of this book based on government reports are so indicated and copyright is claimed for those parts to the extent applicable to compilations of such works.

Independent verification should be sought for any data, advice or recommendations contained in this book. In addition, no responsibility is assumed by the publisher for any injury and/or damage to persons or property arising from any methods, products, instructions, ideas or otherwise contained in this publication.

This publication is designed to provide accurate and authoritative information with regard to the subject matter covered herein. It is sold with the clear understanding that the Publisher is not engaged in rendering legal or any other professional services. If legal or any other expert assistance is required, the services of a competent person should be sought. FROM A DECLARATION OF PARTICIPANTS JOINTLY ADOPTED BY A COMMITTEE OF THE AMERICAN BAR ASSOCIATION AND A COMMITTEE OF PUBLISHERS.

Additional color graphics may be available in the e-book version of this book.

Library of Congress Cataloging-in-Publication Data

ISBN: 978-1-63463-180-8

Published by Nova Science Publishers, Inc. † New York

CONTENTS

PREFACE

Chapter 1 – This report examines human rights issues in the People's Republic of China (PRC), including ongoing rights abuses, legal reforms, and the development of civil society. Major events of the past year include the PRC leadership transition, the Wukan protests over land expropriation, the negotiations that allowed legal advocate Chen Guangcheng to leave China, and the Tibetan self-immolations. Ongoing human rights problems include excessive use of force by public security forces, unlawful detention, torture of detainees, arbitrary use of state security laws against political dissidents and ethnic groups, coercive family planning practices, persecution of unsanctioned religious activity, state control of information, and mistreatment of North Korean refugees. Tibetans, Uighur Muslims, and Falun Gong adherents continue to receive especially harsh treatment.

China's leadership transition has so far provided few indications of a fundamental policy shift on human rights. Nonetheless, many analysts refer to a legitimacy crisis and possible "turning point" after three decades of rapid but uneven economic growth. Some observers sense a shift in public attitudes from an emphasis on economic development and social stability to an eagerness for political reform that would have implications for human rights in China.

Although the ruling Chinese Communist Party (CCP) opposes political pluralism, Chinese society has become more diverse and assertive. Non-governmental organizations are playing a larger role in providing social services and policy input. Social protests are frequent, numerous, and widespread. Economic, social, and demographic changes have given rise to labor unrest. PRC citizens have become increasingly aware of their legal rights, while emerging networks of lawyers, journalists, and activists have advanced the causes of many aggrieved individuals and groups. The media continues to push the boundaries of officially approved discourse, and the Internet has made it impossible for the government to restrict information as fully as before. Some Chinese refer to microblog (*weibo*) sites as the most important public sphere for free speech.

The PRC government has attempted to respond to some popular grievances, develop the legal system, and cautiously support the expansion of civil society. However, it continues to suppress many activists who try to organize mass protests and dissidents who openly question sensitive policies or call for fundamental political change. Many lawyers who take on politically sensitive cases face government reprisals.

Some notable changes to the PRC criminal justice system were announced in the past year. Amendments to the Criminal Procedure Law, which are to go into effect in 2013, reportedly provide for greater protections against torture and coerced confessions, expanded access to legal defense, longer trial deliberations, mandatory appellate hearings, more rigorous judicial review, and greater government oversight of the legal process. In January 2013, the government stated that it planned reforms related to the notorious Re-education Through Labor camps, which hold citizens without trial for non-criminal offenses. Some experts caution that, given China's weak legal system, it is too early to predict whether these reforms will result in significant improvements in rights protections in these areas.

The United States government has developed an array of policy tools aimed at promoting democracy and human rights in China, including sanctions, open criticism of PRC human rights policies, diplomacy, and bilateral dialogue. U.S.-funded Voice of America and Radio Free Asia have made efforts to upgrade their Internet offerings and ensure access in China. Congress has funded democracy, human rights, rule of law, and Internet freedom programs and efforts in China and Tibetan areas of the PRC. Some policy makers contend that U.S. engagement with China has failed to produce meaningful political reform and improvements in human rights conditions. Other experts argue that U.S. engagement has helped to advance economic and social change in China, to develop legal and social foundations for democracy and human rights, and to open channels through which to directly communicate U.S. concerns.

Chapter 2 – The People's Republic of China (PRC) is an authoritarian state in which the Chinese Communist Party (CCP) constitutionally is the paramount authority. CCP members hold almost all top government and security apparatus positions. Ultimate authority rests with the 25-member Political Bureau (Politburo) of the CCP and its seven-member Standing

Committee. China completed its once-in-a-decade leadership transition in March, and Xi Jinping holds the three most powerful positions as CCP general secretary, state president, and chairman of the Central Military Commission. Civilian authorities generally maintained control of the military and internal security forces. Security forces committed human rights abuses.

Repression and coercion, particularly against organizations and individuals involved in civil and political rights advocacy and public interest issues, ethnic minorities, and law firms that took on sensitive cases, were routine. Increasingly officials employed harassment, intimidation, and prosecution of family members and associates to retaliate against rights advocates and defenders. Individuals and groups seen as politically sensitive by authorities continued to face tight restrictions on their freedom to assemble, practice religion, and travel. Authorities resorted to extralegal measures such as enforced disappearance and strict house arrest, including house arrest of family members, to prevent public expression of independent opinions. Authorities implemented new measures to control and censor the internet and particularly targeted bloggers with large numbers of followers, leading some to close their online accounts. Public-interest law firms continued to face harassment, disbarment of legal staff, and closure. There was severe official repression of the freedoms of speech, religion, association, and assembly of ethnic Uighurs in the Xinjiang Uighur Autonomous Region (XUAR) and of ethnic Tibetans in the Tibet Autonomous Region (TAR) and other Tibetan areas. These minorities also faced harsh restrictions on movement. Abuses peaked around high-profile events, such as the visit of foreign officials, national meetings, and commemorations.

As in previous years, citizens did not have the right to change their government, and citizens had limited forms of redress against official abuse. Other human rights problems during the year included extrajudicial killings, including executions without due process; enforced disappearance and incommunicado detention, including prolonged illegal detentions at unofficial holding facilities known as "black jails"; torture and coerced confessions of prisoners; detention and harassment of lawyers, journalists, writers, bloggers, dissidents, petitioners, and others who sought to exercise peacefully their rights under the law; a lack of due process in judicial proceedings; political control of courts and judges; closed trials; the use of administrative detention; restrictions on freedom to assemble, practice religion, and travel; failure to protect refugees and asylum seekers; pressure on other countries to return PRC citizens forcibly; widespread corruption; intense scrutiny of and restrictions on nongovernmental organizations (NGOs); discrimination against women, minorities, and persons with disabilities; a coercive birth-limitation policy that in some cases resulted in forced abortion (sometimes at advanced stages of pregnancy) or forced sterilization; trafficking in persons; prohibitions on independent unions; lack of protection for workers' right to strike; forced and child labor; and poor enforcement of wage, overtime, and occupational safety and health laws.

Although authorities prosecuted a number of abuses of power, particularly with regard to corruption, in many cases the internal disciplinary procedures of the CCP were opaque and only selectively applied to senior officials. Citizens who promoted efforts to combat corruption were themselves detained and arrested. For example, throughout the year, NGO sources reported that authorities arrested at least 29 persons associated with the New Citizens Movement on charges stemming from activities to promote good governance.

Chapter 3 – Since the Commission's examination in 2008 of prison labor issues in the People's Republic of China (PRC), there has been little substantive reduction in the scale and scope of China's broad network of prison labor facilities. These facilities, led by local officials, continue to produce goods intended for export, including online goods and services, on a potentially large scale, in violation of U.S.-China agreements on the exports of prison labor goods to the United States. Further, it is unclear whether the recent abolition of "reeducation through labor" (RTL) and reported release of up to tens of thousands of prisoners will have a significant impact on the prison labor system and export of prison labor products.

Although U.S. representatives in Beijing have continued to engage with their Chinese counterparts regarding suspected prison manufacturing facilities, the pattern of long delays and minimal cooperation by officials in the PRC Ministry of Prisons persists. Allegations of prison labor exports from China to the United States and other countries continue to surface, raising legitimate doubts regarding the effectiveness of current enforcement mechanisms.

In: Human Rights in China
Editor: Kimberly Austin

ISBN: 978-1-63463-180-8
© 2014 Nova Science Publishers, Inc.

Chapter 1

HUMAN RIGHTS IN CHINA AND U.S. POLICY: ISSUES FOR THE 113TH CONGRESS[*]

Thomas Lum

SUMMARY

This report examines human rights issues in the People's Republic of China (PRC), including ongoing rights abuses, legal reforms, and the development of civil society. Major events of the past year include the PRC leadership transition, the Wukan protests over land expropriation, the negotiations that allowed legal advocate Chen Guangcheng to leave China, and the Tibetan self-immolations. Ongoing human rights problems include excessive use of force by public security forces, unlawful detention, torture of detainees, arbitrary use of state security laws against political dissidents and ethnic groups, coercive family planning practices, persecution of unsanctioned religious activity, state control of information, and mistreatment of North Korean refugees. Tibetans, Uighur Muslims, and Falun Gong adherents continue to receive especially harsh treatment.

China's leadership transition has so far provided few indications of a fundamental policy shift on human rights. Nonetheless, many analysts refer to a legitimacy crisis and possible "turning point" after three decades of rapid but uneven economic growth. Some observers sense a shift in public attitudes from an emphasis on economic development and

---

[*] This is an edited, reformatted and augmented version of a Congressional Research Service publication, No. R43000, dated June 19, 2013.

social stability to an eagerness for political reform that would have implications for human rights in China.

Although the ruling Chinese Communist Party (CCP) opposes political pluralism, Chinese society has become more diverse and assertive. Non-governmental organizations are playing a larger role in providing social services and policy input. Social protests are frequent, numerous, and widespread. Economic, social, and demographic changes have given rise to labor unrest. PRC citizens have become increasingly aware of their legal rights, while emerging networks of lawyers, journalists, and activists have advanced the causes of many aggrieved individuals and groups. The media continues to push the boundaries of officially approved discourse, and the Internet has made it impossible for the government to restrict information as fully as before. Some Chinese refer to microblog (*weibo*) sites as the most important public sphere for free speech.

The PRC government has attempted to respond to some popular grievances, develop the legal system, and cautiously support the expansion of civil society. However, it continues to suppress many activists who try to organize mass protests and dissidents who openly question sensitive policies or call for fundamental political change. Many lawyers who take on politically sensitive cases face government reprisals.

Some notable changes to the PRC criminal justice system were announced in the past year. Amendments to the Criminal Procedure Law, which are to go into effect in 2013, reportedly provide for greater protections against torture and coerced confessions, expanded access to legal defense, longer trial deliberations, mandatory appellate hearings, more rigorous judicial review, and greater government oversight of the legal process. In January 2013, the government stated that it planned reforms related to the notorious Re-education Through Labor camps, which hold citizens without trial for non-criminal offenses. Some experts caution that, given China's weak legal system, it is too early to predict whether these reforms will result in significant improvements in rights protections in these areas.

The United States government has developed an array of policy tools aimed at promoting democracy and human rights in China, including sanctions, open criticism of PRC human rights policies, diplomacy, and bilateral dialogue. U.S.-funded Voice of America and Radio Free Asia have made efforts to upgrade their Internet offerings and ensure access in China. Congress has funded democracy, human rights, rule of law, and Internet freedom programs and efforts in China and Tibetan areas of the PRC. Some policy makers contend that U.S. engagement with China has failed to produce meaningful political reform and improvements in human rights conditions. Other experts argue that U.S. engagement has helped to advance economic and social change in China, to develop legal and social foundations for democracy and human rights, and to open channels through which to directly communicate U.S. concerns.

OVERVIEW

Human rights conditions in the People's Republic of China (PRC) remain a central issue in U.S.- China relations. For many U.S. policy-makers, China's political development represents a test of the success of U.S. policy toward China. Some analysts contend that the U.S. policy of cultivating diplomatic, economic, and cultural ties with the PRC has failed to produce meaningful political reforms, and that without fundamental progress in this area, the bilateral relationship will remain rocky. They add that U.S. efforts to promote human rights and democracy in the PRC are constrained by the overarching policy of U.S. engagement with China, which includes other U.S. interests and values. The U.S. government has developed a comprehensive array of tactics and programs aimed at promoting democracy, human rights, and the rule of law in China, although their effects have been felt primarily along the margins of the PRC political system. Other experts argue that U.S. engagement has helped to accelerate economic and social change and create the necessary conditions for political reform in China. They hold that Washington has little direct leverage over Beijing's internal policies, and that sanctions and efforts to link the bilateral relationship to improvements in human rights in China have not been very effective.[1]

Many observers argue that violations of civil liberties and cases of political and religious persecution in China have increased in recent years, the leadership remains authoritarian, and economic development, based in part upon trade with the United States, has strengthened the Communist government rather than empowered the people. Other analysts and many Chinese citizens contend that, at the same time, economic and social freedoms have grown considerably, the government's control over most aspects of people's lives has receded, opportunities for providing opinions on policy have increased, and rights activism has sprouted. Disagreements over whether progress has been made often stem from differences over which indicators are emphasized, such as central government policies, local government actions, civil society, or short-term versus long-term trends. In many ways, growing government restrictions on political, religious, and other freedoms and greater assertion of civil rights have occurred simultaneously.

Assessing Human Rights Conditions in China

Human rights conditions in the PRC reflect multiple and conflicting trends. The government is led by the Chinese Communist Party (CCP), whose rule is referenced in the preamble to China's Constitution, and the legislative and judicial branches of government lack real power to check the CCP and the state. The PRC Constitution (Article 35) guarantees many rights, including the freedoms of speech, press, assembly, demonstration, and religious belief. However, the government restricts these rights in practice. The CCP regards these rights as subordinate to its own authority and to the policy goals of maintaining social stability and state security, promoting economic development, and providing for economic and social rights. The PRC leadership frequently denounces foreign criticisms of its human rights policies as interference in China's internal affairs, and asserts that perspectives on human rights vary according to a country's level of economic development and social system.

During the past decade, the PRC government has developed along the lines of what some scholars call "responsive authoritarianism."[2] It has striven to become more legalistic, accountable, and responsive. The government has made some progress in enacting laws aimed at curbing some of the most egregious human rights abuses. In the past year, the state enacted new laws that may provide better protections for some criminal defendants and pledged to reform the notorious Reeducation Through Labor camps.

However, the government has rejected political reforms that might undermine its monopoly on power, and continued to respond forcefully to signs and instances of social instability, autonomous social organization, and independent political activity. The state has continued to crack down upon unsanctioned religious, ethnic, and labor activity and organizations, political dissidents, and rights lawyers. Government authorities have imposed particularly harsh policies against Tibetans, Uighurs, and Falun Gong adherents. Chinese leaders have tolerated some public criticism and protest against government officials and policies, particularly at the local level, but have also arrested protest leaders. Communist Party and state officials retain a significant degree of arbitrary authority, and corruption has negated many efforts to improve governance.

Citizen Activism

Awareness of civil and legal rights among Chinese citizens, in some ways promoted by the government, continues to grow, while a small but increasing number of activists, lawyers, journalists, and others have continued to champion human rights causes.[3] Despite strict controls on civil and political rights, many Chinese citizens have become more assertive in claiming rights that exist on paper and have developed a greater sense of political efficacy. Some of them have engaged in public demonstrations against mistreatment by local authorities and employers, invoking the rule of law and expressing their views on the Internet. They have taken advantage of new opportunities to utilize the legal system, comment on public policies, and participate in civil society. According to one specialist, "broad public participation in activist causes has become one of the most potent political dynamics in China today."[4]

China's rising middle class has become more demanding of government. The middle class's growing involvement in demonstrations on local issues is particularly significant, given its effectiveness in articulating interests and its importance to the central government's legitimacy. Nonetheless, the government is unlikely to support radical political change in the near future, some experts say. Surveys show that urban Chinese, the core of the middle class, feel strongly about clean and responsive government, support civil liberties, and are politically aware. However, in many ways, they are dependent upon the state for their material well-being and may be somewhat politically conservative. Most urban residents are not prone to agitate for democracy if they perceive that their economic needs are being met. They have been careful not to jeopardize their hard-won economic gains, and have expressed some fear of grassroots democracy.[5] A survey commissioned by the Pew Research Center found that Chinese perceptions of the U.S.-China relationship are significantly more negative in 2012 than in 2010. However, a slightly greater percentage likes or admires "American ideas about democracy" in 2012 (52%) than in 2010 (48%). This is especially true of urban, young, educated, and affluent Chinese.[6]

A "Turning Point?"

China's once-in-a-decade leadership transition, which was completed in March 2013, has provided few indications of a policy shift on human rights. Most analysts agree that it is unlikely that there will be significant changes soon, as the new leaders, Party Secretary Xi Jinping and Premier Li Keqiang, consolidate their power. Two Party leaders considered to be political reformers, Wang Yang and Li Yuanchao, were not selected as members of the leadership core, the seven-member Standing Committee of the Politburo, although Li Yuanchao was awarded the largely ceremonial post of state vice president. As incidents of social protest continue, the government has expanded funding for public security and emphasized the need to improve "social management." However, some observers argue that due to the greater political assertiveness of the Chinese people compared to a decade ago, the government likely will seek to avoid a popular backlash, by limiting repressive actions largely to selected key activists, dissidents, and groups.

Many analysts refer to a legitimacy crisis and possible "turning point" for the CCP after three decades of rapid but uneven economic growth. Some observers sense a shift in public attitude from an emphasis on economic development and social stability to a readiness for political reform.[7] Disagreements reportedly exist within the Party regarding how to address problems related to economic inequality, political development, corruption, social welfare, and the environment. In the past year, Party members, intellectuals, lawyers, and journalists issued several high-profile demands for political change, including calls for constitutional government, an open letter signed by 72 scholars urging democratic reform within the existing political system, and a petition to the National People's Congress supporting ratification of the International Covenant on Civil and Political Rights.[8]

SELECTED EVENTS AND DEVELOPMENTS OF THE PAST YEAR

A number of events of the past year indicate the evolving relationship between the PRC state and a changing society. As incidents of social protest have increased, the government has bolstered funding and staff for social control efforts. In many cases of public protest against violations of economic rights, such as property and labor rights, the central government has attempted to strike a neutral or sympathetic tone, particularly when corrupt local officials were involved. However, it has not directly addressed the concentrations of power that lie at the root of the problems. Although direct elections for village committees, instituted in the 1980s, sowed the seeds for a modicum of democratic decision-making in China, their progression to higher levels of government has stalled for over two decades.[9] Recent efforts by citizens to rejuvenate the process illustrated how many Chinese embrace the notion of grassroots democracy, and how wary the CCP is of losing political control. The events surrounding blind legal advocate Chen Guangcheng in May 2012 showed how the PRC government has attempted to silence outspoken rights advocates and dissidents, but also how activist networks have managed to survive in its shadow. (For more on Chen's case, see "Chen Guangcheng" below.) Finally, the Tibetan immolations reflect Beijing's hard line against some ethnic and religious groups, despite demonstrating some flexibility in other areas.

Social Management

Public protests occur on a daily basis in China, although they largely focus on local economic issues rather than national political ones. Estimates of the number "mass incidents" vary, from roughly 90,000 to 180,000 annually during the past several years.[10] Typical sources of unrest include forcible evictions of urban residents, poor factory conditions and unpaid wages, farmers facing environmental degradation brought about by industrial development, migrants experiencing physical abuse by "urban management officers" (*chengguan*), and arbitrary or heavy-handed treatment of small enterprises. According to some analysts, activism reflects an increasingly assertive citizenry, armed with an understanding of the law and empowered by social media and other forms of online communication and news.[11] Other groups who demonstrated during the past year include women, gays and lesbians, the disabled, sex workers, and advocates for HIV/AIDS awareness.

In recent years, PRC leaders have focused on strengthening institutions that address social unrest. In 2011, the Central Commission for Comprehensive Social Management, which oversees public security, expanded its presence from 29 party and government departments and agencies to 40.[12] The Chinese government increased funding for "public safety" by 9% in 2013, to $124 billion.[13] During the period of the CCP Congress in November 2012, in which the next generation of leaders was announced, human rights groups reported a crackdown on petitioners, dissidents, academics, and activists. They asserted that up to 100,000 people were affected, and two petitioners— ordinary citizens seeking official redress of their grievances—were believed to have died in custody.[14]

Wukan

The seven-month-long unrest in Wukan, Guangdong province, symbolized the heavily skewed power structure in China, growing incidents of mass protest, and the range of responses from the PRC government. The province's Party Secretary at the time, Wang Yang, received praise for helping to resolve the tensions in a relatively flexible and sympathetic manner, unlike many government responses elsewhere, and in way that could be seen as an example for other disputes.[15] In September 2011, Wukan villagers protested the taking of agricultural land for development and the lack of adequate compensation. They stormed government offices, resulting in the Party Secretary and other leaders fleeing the village. The local government offered to negotiate, but subsequently arrested protest leaders and attempted to forcibly take control of the village. The death of a protest leader in custody (Xue Jinbo) further inflamed passions. Village authorities asserted that he died of heart failure while family members claimed that he had been severely beaten. Villagers then blocked roads and engaged in a 10-day standoff with security forces. The provincial government stepped in, promising to investigate the land dispute, release the remaining three leaders, and to allow free and open elections for the village committee, which has power over the sale of collectively owned land. In a sign of growing international interest, the U.S. government sent an observer to the poll. In March 2012, Wukan villagers elected an entirely new committee, complaining that the former members had been involved in corrupt development schemes and ruled like "local emperors."[16] A year after the unrest began, however, some villagers complained to the foreign media that local authorities still had not returned their land.[17]

Local Elections

PRC citizens can directly elect officials to village committees and assemblies and to the more powerful township, county, and municipal district people's congresses. By law, any organization or group of 10 persons or more can nominate a candidate to the local people's congress. Although voters generally have a choice of candidates and candidates are not required to be Communist Party members, CCP election committees may disqualify candidates at any level, and they effectively control most candidate lists. A growing number of citizens have run as "independent" candidates for township and district people's congresses, including academics, college students, journalists, bloggers, leaders of non-governmental organizations (NGOs), private entrepreneurs, lawyers, and farmers. Many of them have conducted their election campaigns through such media as the Internet and microblogging (*weibo*). Many candidates have experienced government harassment, such as surveillance, intimidation, or detention, forcing some of them to quit. Local authorities reportedly also have pressured nominators, family members, and employers.[18]

Chen Guangcheng[19]

The case of the blind legal advocate Chen Guangcheng exemplifies China's treatment of political activists, including Chen's prolonged house arrest, lack of due process, and physical abuse. Chen, a self-trained legal advocate, challenged local authorities to uphold China's laws and regulations in the areas of disability rights and family planning. In 2005, he attempted to organize a class-action lawsuit on behalf of victims of forced abortions and sterilizations. Local authorities ultimately charged Chen with disturbing public order and disrupting traffic. In 2006, Chen, who had no legal representation at his trial, was sentenced to over four years in prison. After Chen completed his sentence in 2010, he was placed under extra-judicial house arrest. His wife's movements also were restricted. The couple's son was sent to live with the parents of Chen's wife, and, for a time, their young daughter was prevented from attending school. Cell phone communication to and from their home was blocked. In 2011, security agents allegedly beat Chen and his wife in their house after they smuggled out a video, later posted online, in which they described the conditions of their forced confinement.

In the early morning of April 22, 2012, after 19 months of confinement in his house, Chen, by now well-known in China and abroad, escaped his heavily guarded home and village under cover of darkness. Rights activists and others, including He Peirong and Guo Yushan, allegedly helped transport Chen from his village in Yinan County, Shandong province to Beijing. Chen was reported to be under the protection of the U.S. Embassy on April 27, days before then-Secretary of State Hillary Clinton was to arrive in the PRC capital to attend the annual U.S.-China Security and Economic Dialogue. Chen stayed at the U.S. Embassy for six days before being transferred to a Beijing hospital to get treatment for a broken foot, sustained during his escape, and a stomach ailment. After three weeks of tense negotiations over his fate, Chinese leaders agreed to allow the legal advocate to leave the country with his wife and children for the United States to study law.

In November 2012, the People's Court of Yinan County sentenced Chen Kegui, Chen Guangcheng's nephew, to 39 months in prison for injuring a government official during the morning of April 22. Chen Kegui alleged that he was defending himself and his parents as the official and government agents violently stormed his house in search of his uncle. Chen Kegui reportedly was denied legal counsel of his choice and other forms of due process.[20]

Tibetan Self-Immolations

The PRC government has maintained an increased security presence in the Tibet Autonomous Region (TAR) and other Tibetan areas of China since the unrest of March 2008. Since 2009, about 120 Tibetans within China reportedly have set fire to themselves to protest PRC policies.[21] Most of the self-immolations have taken place in and around the Kirti Monastery in Aba County, Sichuan Province as well as in other Tibetan areas of Sichuan, Gansu, and Qinghai provinces. PRC leaders have blamed Tibet's exiled spiritual leader, the Dalai Lama, Tibetan separatists, foreign groups, and other alleged instigators for stirring unrest in Tibetan areas and encouraging self-immolations. An opinion issued by PRC judicial and law enforcement bodies stated that citizens involved in self-immolations would be held criminally liable. In February 2013, police in Gansu province reportedly arrested five Tibetans, who they alleged persuaded three people to set themselves on fire "at the behest of foreign forces."[22] In a statement, the U.S. Special Coordinator for Tibetan Issues Maria Otero asserted that "The United States is deeply concerned and saddened by the continuing violence in Tibetan areas of China and the increasing frequency of self-immolations by Tibetans.... We call on the Chinese government to permit Tibetans to express their grievances freely, publicly, peacefully, and without fear of retribution."[23]

ONGOING HUMAN RIGHTS ISSUES

As discussed above, major, ongoing human rights violations in China include the following: excessive use of violence by security forces and their proxies; unlawful and abusive detention; torture; arbitrary use of state security laws against political dissidents; coercive family planning policies; and state control of information. Other violations include harassment and persecution of people involved in unsanctioned religious activities, including worship in unregistered Protestant "house churches" and Catholic churches that express loyalty to the Pope; and mistreatment and deportation of North Korean refugees.

The following list provides a selection of specific human rights issues in China, some of which are discussed at greater length elsewhere in this report:[24]

- Harassment, beatings by public security forces and plainclothes agents, house arrest, and unlawful detentions of petitioners, protest leaders, human rights attorneys, journalists, dissidents, and others.
- Unlawful killings of persons in state custody.
- Physical abuse and the use of torture by the state against political detainees and criminal suspects, often resulting in forced confessions or renunciations of faith.
- Arbitrary use of state security laws against political dissidents, Tibetans, Uighur Muslims, Internet bloggers, and others.
- Sporadic reports of coercive abortions, forced sterilizations, and other related, unlawful government actions against women.
- Strict controls over and punishments for public speech, discussion, and reporting of politically sensitive topics, such as the Tiananmen events of 1989, Taiwan relations, Tibet, Falun Gong, and the legitimacy of the Chinese Communist Party.
- Harassment and arrests of Christians worshipping in unofficial churches.
- Persecution of Falun Gong adherents.
- Repatriation of North Korean nationals residing in China, who likely face severe forms of punishment after returning North Korea, in violation of the U.N. Refugee Convention and its protocols.

Prisoners of Conscience and Extrajudicial Detention

The Dui Hua Foundation, a non-profit organization that aims to bring clemency and better treatment to at-risk detainees through the promotion of universally recognized human rights and dialogue with China, estimates that there are 20,000 to 30,000 political and religious prisoners or prisoners of conscience in the PRC.[25] They are held in prisons, Re-education Through

Labor camps, and forms of arbitrary detention. Principal categories of detainees include those deemed guilty of "endangering state security" (ESS), members of "cults" such as Falun Gong, Tibetans, and Uighurs. The number of people tried for endangering state security in 2011 (974) represented a decline of 20% compared to 2010. Nonetheless, ESS levels remain high compared to the years prior to 2008-2009, when social unrest erupted in Tibet and Xinjiang.[26]

Re-Education through Labor

Re-education Through Labor (RETL), an administrative measure, empowers police to sentence persons found guilty of minor or *non-criminal* offenses, such as petty theft, prostitution, unlawful religious activity, and "disrupting social order," to a maximum of three to four years in labor camps without trial. According to some estimates, between 2% and 10% of the RETL population is sent there for political reasons. Many Falun Gong adherents were sent to RETL camps during the height of the crackdown on their group a decade ago, at one time reportedly constituting from one-quarter to one-half of all detainees.[27] Estimates of the RETL population vary, from roughly 160,000 to 260,000 persons.[28] According to one source, drug offenders constitute the largest group in the RETL system, or about 200,000 people.[29]

For the past decade, many Chinese scholars and government officials have openly advocated reforming the RETL system. In 2012, Tang Hui, the mother of an 11-year old rape victim, was sentenced to 18 months in an RETL facility in Hunan province after she protested the conduct of local officials in the resolution of her daughter's case. The story provoked an outpouring of public support for both Tang and reform of RETL.[30] Reforms may include establishing some procedural rights, providing for access to counsel, and limiting sentences, according to some experts. In November 2011, pilot reform projects were launched in four Chinese cities. In February 2013, the Yunnan provincial government eliminated some offenses considered grounds for RETL detention, including "causing unrest while making complaints about government officials" and "smearing the image of top officials." The removal of these offenses appears to reduce the risks of punishment for people who criticize the government.[31]

In January 2013, Meng Jianzhu, the newly appointed head of the CCP Political and Legal Affairs Committee, reportedly declared in a meeting of judicial officials that the government would stop sending people to RETL camps by the end of the year. However, the state press then changed the wording of the announcement to "reform" of the system.[32] According to some analysts, the state's backtracking on Meng's remarks reflects a concern about how to handle current detainees as well as future offenders and politically troublesome cases, and disagreement among the Chinese leadership about how to proceed. Some human rights experts fear that reforms may be largely cosmetic. They argue that the government may criminalize hitherto non-criminal acts, resulting in an increase in the formal prison population. Furthermore, other forms of informal detention may still be used.[33]

"Black Jails" and Other Forms of Arbitrary Detention

China's system of formal and informal prisons and detention centers reportedly perpetrates some of the most egregious human rights violations, particularly toward citizens who actively opposed government actions and policy. Many political dissidents accused of violating state security laws have been held incommunicado for long periods. Many petitioners—generally people from rural areas who travel to Beijing to seek redress for local government abuses and misconduct—have been sent to secret detention centers, or "black jails," where they lack legal protections and face a variety of abuses. Many of these centers are operated by the governments of the petitioners' home provinces in an attempt to prevent them from taking their complaints to the central government. Many petitioners, rights activists, Falun Gong practitioners, underground religious worshippers, and others also have been held in psychiatric (*ankang*) hospitals for the criminally insane, where they reportedly have been forced to take medications and subjected to other human rights violations. In 2011, the Beijing municipal government reportedly launched a crackdown on black jails. In December 2012, tens of thousands of petitioners reportedly were suddenly released from a detention center in Beijing.[34] In February 2013, a Beijing court sentenced 10 people who operated a black jail for the Henan provincial government to prison.[35]

Imprisoned Nobel Laureate Liu Xiaobo

In October 2010, the Nobel Committee awarded Liu Xiaobo, a longtime political dissident, activist, and writer, the Nobel Peace Prize for his "long and non-violent struggle for fundamental human rights." In December 2008, Liu helped draft "Charter '08" commemorating the 60th anniversary of the United Nations' adoption of the Universal Declaration of Human Rights.[36] The document, signed by 300 Chinese citizens and posted on the Internet, called for human rights and fundamental changes in China's political system. The Charter eventually garnered roughly 10,000 additional signatures online. The PRC government shut down the Charter's website, reportedly harassed, interrogated, and denied career opportunities to dozens of signatories, and arrested Liu. In December 2009, a Beijing court sentenced Liu to 11 years in prison on charges of "inciting subversion of state power." He is the world's only imprisoned Nobel laureate. Although she has been accused of no crimes, Liu Xiaobo's wife, Liu Xia, remains under house arrest in Beijing. In June 2013, a court outside of Beijing sentenced Liu Xia's brother, Liu Hui, to 11 years in prison for fraud, which some observers view as a trumped up charge.

Americans Imprisoned in China

The cases of American citizens convicted of national security-related and commercial crimes in China have periodically caused friction in the U.S.-China relationship. Xue Feng, a U.S. citizen born in China, was arrested in Beijing in 2007 on charges related to his acquisition of a Chinese database on China's oil industry, while working for an American firm. In July 2010, after having been held incommunicado for a period and allegedly tortured, Xue was sentenced to eight years in prison for providing state secrets to foreigners. Xue's term was reduced by 10 months in 2012; he is due to be released in January 2015. Xue stated that he had believed the database to be commercially available.[37] Dong Wei, a naturalized U.S. citizen from China, was detained in 2003 while in Guangzhou as part of a Louisiana trade delegation. He was sentenced in 2005 to 13 years in prison on the charge of espionage (spying for Taiwan). His sentence was reduced by a total of four years. Dong reportedly was released in 2012.[38]

Rights Attorneys and the Rights of the Accused

Lawyers who take on politically sensitive cases often face reprisals, including the forced closure of law offices, suspension or cancellation of law licenses, unlawful detention, beatings by plainclothes agents, house arrest, and prison terms. In 2012, new regulations required attorneys to take an oath of allegiance to the Communist Party when applying for or renewing licenses, and since 2008, the CCP has established cells in most law firms.[39] Jiang Tianyong, an attorney who defended Chen Guangcheng in 2005, reportedly was apprehended by security agents, detained, and beaten when he tried to visit Chen during the diplomatic standoff over Chen's fate in May 2012. Ni Yulan, a rights lawyer specializing in land rights and the legal defense of home owners facing eviction, was sentenced to two years and eight months in prison in 2012 for fraud and "picking quarrels and provoking trouble," while her husband was sentenced to two years in jail. Ni allegedly was permanently disabled while in police custody for rights activism in 2008, and is confined to a wheel chair.

Despite amendments to the PRC Law on Lawyers in 2008, which removed some restrictions on lawyers' access to clients and allowed for greater confidentiality between attorneys and their clients, the legal system remains heavily biased against criminal defendants and their counsel. There is no presumption of innocence and a heavy reliance on confessions to establish guilt, often leading to physical abuse, although recent criminal justice reforms may offer some rights protections. Roughly 70% of criminal defendants in China go to trial without a lawyer, and the conviction rate for criminal defendants is over 99%, according to recent reports.[40] Defense lawyers complain of the "three difficulties" of gaining access to detained clients, reviewing prosecutors' case files, and collecting evidence. Article 306 of China's Criminal Law, which makes it a crime to fabricate evidence or induce a witness to change his or her testimony, often has been invoked to deter defense lawyers from gathering evidence and to prosecute attorneys who had advised clients to recant confessions obtained through torture.[41]

Religious Freedom

The extent of religious freedom and activity in China varies widely by religion, region, and jurisdiction. Hundreds of millions of Chinese openly practice one of five officially recognized religions (Buddhism, Protestantism, Roman Catholicism, Daoism, and Islam). Article X of the PRC Constitution protects "normal" religious activities and those that do not "disrupt public order, impair the health of citizens or interfere with the educational system of the state." Religious organizations in China are playing growing roles in providing social and charitable services. However, the PRC government has imposed especially strict policies and measures upon many unofficial Christian churches, Tibetan Buddhists, Uighur Muslims, and Falun Gong practitioners, largely due to the potential for these groups to become independent social forces or cultivate foreign support. The Department of State has identified China as a "country of particular concern" (CPC) for "particularly severe violations of religious freedom" for 13 consecutive years (2000-2012). In April 2013, U.S. Ambassador at Large for International Religious Freedom Suzan Johnson Cook traveled to China to discuss religious freedom issues.[42]

Christians

Christian worship in China, both within official bodies and outside of them, has continued to grow. According to some estimates, roughly 30 million Chinese Christians worship in state-sanctioned churches, while 40 million to 70 million Chinese Christians practice their faith in unregistered, mostly Protestant congregations.[43] Many Chinese Protestants have rejected the official church, known as the Three Self Patriotic Movement, for political or theological reasons, while some independent or "house" churches claim that their attempts to apply for official status have been rejected by local Religious Affairs Bureaus.[44] Although in many localities, unsanctioned religious congregations may receive little state interference, they still are vulnerable to arbitrary restrictions. In many areas, house churches face harassment by government authorities, their leaders have been beaten, detained, and imprisoned, and their properties have been destroyed.

A number of high profile cases illustrate the tensions between the state and unregistered religious organizations. Local governments have attempted to forcibly prevent followers of the 50,000-member Linfen Church in Shanxi province and the 1,000-member Shouwang church in Beijing from gathering and building or renting their own places of worship. Members of these congregations have experienced arrest, detention, and punishment at work. In 2012, followers of the Hotan church in Xinjiang were forcibly prevented from gathering. The local public security bureau reportedly raided the church and seized property and harassed and temporarily detained church leaders. Local officials stated that this was due to "Xinjiang's special situation."[45]

Catholics in China are divided between those who follow the Pope and those who belong to the official Chinese Catholic Patriotic Association (CCPA), which does not recognize Papal authority. Beijing and the Vatican have long been at odds regarding which side has the authority to appoint bishops. Most Chinese bishops have received approval from both Beijing and the Holy See, but since 2010, the CCPA has ordained five bishops without Rome's approval, further aggravating relations between Beijing and the Vatican. A controversy erupted in July 2012, when Ma Daqin, a new bishop approved by both Beijing and the Vatican, renounced his ties to the CCPA in his first sermon. The PRC government responded by placing Ma under house arrest and stripping him of his title. At least 40 unregistered Chinese bishops reportedly are under surveillance, in hiding, being detained, confined to their homes, or have disappeared, according to the Congressional-Executive Commission on China (CECC).[46]

China Aid Association, an organization that monitors human rights abuses against Christians in the PRC, reported that the persecution of Christians has worsened in the past several years. Beginning in 2010, China's State Administration for Religious Affairs renewed government efforts to weaken independent Christian churches by bringing their members into state-sanctioned churches, preventing large congregations from gathering, and restricting the movements and activities of their leaders. According to China Aid, in 2011, 1,200 Christians were detained and four were sentenced.[47]

Tibetans[48]

Although the PRC has controlled the Tibetan Autonomous Region and other Tibetan areas since 1951, it continues to face resistance to its rule, with some Tibetans viewing Chinese government policies as a challenge to their religion, culture, and identity. Increasingly expansive controls on Tibetan religious life and practice have served to further feed discontent. These policies include a heightened official and security presence within monasteries, increased surveillance, political education campaigns in religious institutions and villages which pressure Tibetans to denounce the Dalai Lama, and restrictions on the mass media, movement, and travel abroad.[49] The State Department reports "serious human rights abuses including extrajudicial killings, torture, arbitrary arrests, extrajudicial detention, and house arrests" in the region.[50] The CECC has obtained records of 626 Tibetan political prisoners and detainees, the vast majority of whom were apprehended following the civil unrest of March 2008.[51]

Other sources of grievance for many Tibetans are the domination of the local economy by Han Chinese (the majority ethnic group in China) and the adverse environmental effects of Beijing's development projects in the TAR. By contrast, many Hans believe that PRC government policies have brought positive economic and social development to the region. Hans form a minority in the TAR, about 8% of the total population of 3 million people, according to official Chinese census figures.[52] However, some observers believe that Hans constitute over half of the population of Lhasa, the Tibetan capital.[53]

2008 Protests and Their Aftermath

On March 11, 2008, the 49th anniversary of the 1959 Tibetan uprising against Chinese rule, approximately 300 Buddhist monks demonstrated peacefully to demand the release of Tibetan prisoners of conscience. These demonstrations sparked other protests by monks and other Tibetans demanding independence from China or greater autonomy. On March 15, demonstrations in Lhasa turned violent as Tibetan protesters confronted PRC police and burned shops and property owned by Hans. Other Tibetan protests erupted in Tibetan areas of neighboring provinces.

The PRC government has maintained an increased security presence in the TAR and other Tibetan areas of the PRC since 2008. Crackdowns have been particularly intense during politically sensitive periods, such as last year's 18th Congress of the Chinese Communist Party. China's leaders have bolstered efforts to spur economic development in Tibet, provide greater economic opportunities for Tibetans, and improve social services. However, they have displayed little, if any, flexibility on the questions of greater autonomy and religious freedom.

As mentioned above, since 2009, about 120 Tibetans within China are reported to have set fire to themselves to protest PRC policies. Chinese leaders have blamed the Dalai Lama, Tibetan separatists, foreign groups, and other alleged instigators for causing restiveness in Tibetan areas and encouraging self-immolations. Chinese courts have arrested nearly 20 people for allegedly inciting Tibetans to set themselves on fire. The Dalai Lama has described the self-immolations as "very, very sad" and the product of "a very desperate situation." He has declined to either endorse or condemn them, but has questioned "how much effect [there is] from such drastic actions."[54]

Beijing-Dalai Lama Dialogue

The ninth round of talks between Beijing and representatives of the Dalai Lama since 2002, which took place in January 2010, failed to bring about any fundamental progress on the issue of greater autonomy for Tibet. The Dalai Lama's representatives pledged respect for the authority of the PRC central government, but continued to push for "genuine autonomy" for the Tibetan people. Both sides acknowledged that the meetings produced no breakthroughs. Lodi Gyari, the Special Envoy of the Dalai Lama who led nine rounds of talks between 2002 and 2010, resigned in 2012, citing frustration at the lack of progress or a "positive response" by the Chinese government. However, he continued to view the dialogue process as the "only way forward for Tibet, in the absence of other viable options."[55]

In April 2011, Tibetan exiles in India elected a Harvard academic, Lobsang Sangay, as their new prime minister. He assumed some of the political duties of the Dalai Lama, who remains as the Tibetan spiritual leader but relinquished his political role. The Chinese government has vowed not to conduct any talks with the new prime minister and his government, arguing that they represent an illegal organization.

U.S. Policy Toward Tibet

The Tibetan Policy Act of 2002 (P.L. 107-228) directs the executive branch to encourage the PRC government to enter into a dialogue with the Dalai Lama or his representatives; call for the release of Tibetan political and religious prisoners in China; support economic development, cultural preservation, environmental sustainability, and other objectives in Tibet; and carry out other activities to "support the aspirations of the Tibetan people to safeguard their distinct identity."[56] In July 2011, President Obama met with the Dalai Lama for the second time at the White House, despite strong objections from Beijing. The President emphasized the importance of the human rights of Tibetans in China as well as their unique religious, cultural, and linguistic traditions. He stressed that Tibet is a part of China, praised the Dalai Lama's commitment to nonviolence and his "Middle Way" approach, and encouraged dialogue between the Dalai Lama's representatives and Beijing, while also emphasizing the importance of U.S.-China cooperation.

Uighur Muslims

In the past decade, Chinese authorities have carried out especially harsh religious and ethnic policies against Uighurs, a predominantly Muslim Turkic ethnic group living primarily in China's far northwestern Xinjiang Uighur Autonomous Region (XUAR).[57] Once the predominant ethnic group in the region, Xinjiang's 8.5 million Uighurs now constitute an estimated 40% of the population as many Han have migrated there, particularly to the regional capital, Urumqi.[58] The PRC government asserts that many Muslims in China, including Uighurs, receive preferential treatment due to special policies toward minority groups, that PRC economic policies have benefitted Uighurs, and that firm religious and ethnic policies are necessary to prevent terrorism. In 2010, China's top leadership held the first "work forum" focused on the XUAR. The forum produced an ambitious economic development plan for the region, but did not address longstanding Uighur political and religious grievances.

The PRC government has often conflated the religious and cultural practices of Uighurs in Xinjiang with subversive activities or the "three evils of religious extremism, splittism, and terrorism." It claims that the East Turkestan Islamic Movement (ETIM), a Uighur organization that advocates the creation of an independent Uighur Islamic state, was responsible for terrorist attacks in China and has ties to Al Qaeda.[59] In 2011, Xinjiang courts tried 414 cases of endangering state security, up 10% over the previous year.[60]

Uighur and human rights groups have long complained of PRC religious policies that constrain the training and role of imams, the celebration of Ramadan, and participation in the hajj. According to these groups, Uighur children are forbidden from entering mosques and studying the Koran and government workers and teachers are not allowed to openly practice Islam. Other grievances include the loss of ethnic identity, including restrictions on Uighur-language education, economic discrimination, and the lack of consultation on policy. Government efforts to rebuild the ancient heart of Kashgar have angered many Uighurs. Although PRC officials argue that redevelopment is designed to improve public sanitation, provide modern structures, and create better housing, many Kashgar residents say that the new plan is aimed at controlling the local population and will result in the further destruction of Uighur culture.[61]

2009 Ethnic Unrest

On July 5, 2009, an estimated several hundred to a few thousand Uighur demonstrators gathered peacefully in Urumqi to demand that PRC authorities prosecute those responsible for the deaths of two Uighur men involved in a brawl between Han and Uighur factory workers in Guangdong province. Paramilitary police reportedly attacked the demonstrators after they refused to disperse, which eventually provoked a riot and acts of violence against government property, Han residents, and Han shops. In response, bands of Han sought retribution against Uighurs.

Following the 2009 civil strife, the regional government implemented a "Religious Strike Hard Campaign" and further restricted religious activity, speech, assembly, information, and international communication in Uighur areas of western China. The government blocked Internet traffic in the XUAR for 10 months. Beijing blamed Uighur "separatists" and exile groups for plotting the turmoil, particularly the World Uygur Congress led by exiled Uighur businesswoman, leader, and former political prisoner Rebiya Kadeer, who now lives in the United States. Two of Kadeer's sons, Alim Abdireyim and Ablikim Abdireyim, are serving jail sentences in Xinjiang for tax evasion and "engaging in secessionist activities."[62]

2013 Violent Clash

On April 23, 2013, a reported 21 people, including police personnel, members of a community watch patrol, and six Uighurs alleged to be part of a terrorist group, died in a clash in western Xinjiang near the city of Kashgar. Local officials claimed that the Uighur group possessed extremist religious literature and bomb-making materials. PRC authorities, who asserted the Uighur group attacked the community watch officers and a police station after their bomb-making materials were discovered, arrested 19 Uighur suspects. Uighur exile groups questioned the PRC government's version of events, saying that it often uses claims of terrorism to justify excessive security measures. Some Uighurs at the scene reportedly claimed that the violence occurred after local public security forces fired into a crowd that was protesting ongoing police harassment, killing a Uighur youth. The U.S. State Department expressed regret at the loss of life and urged the Chinese government to take steps to reduce tensions in Xinjiang and to "provide all Chinese citizens, including Uighurs, the due process protections to which they're entitled." China's Foreign Ministry criticized the United States for "continually refusing to condemn violent terrorism incidents, and instead, making wild accusations about Chinese policy toward ethnic minorities."[63]

Falun Gong

Falun Gong combines an exercise regimen with meditation, moral values, and spiritual beliefs. The practice is derived from *qigong*, a set of movements said to stimulate the flow of *qi*—vital energies or "life forces"—throughout the body, Buddhist and Daoist concepts, and precepts formulated by Falun Gong's founder Li Hongzhi.[64] The spiritual exercise reportedly gained tens of millions of adherents across China in the late 1990s. On April 25, 1999, thousands of adherents gathered in Beijing to protest the government's growing restrictions on their activities. Following a crackdown that began in the summer of 1999 and deepened in intensity over a period of roughly two years, the group, which the government labeled a dangerous or evil cult, ceased to practice or agitate in the open. Nonetheless, practitioners continued to gather in secret and the state continued to suppress them. Although the group reportedly declined in importance as a security risk after 2004, overseas Falun Gong organizations claimed that public security forces intensified their persecution of Falun Gong during the 2008 Beijing Olympics, the 2009 Shanghai World Expo, and the 2010 Asian Games in Guangzhou.[65] In 2010, PRC authorities reportedly launched a three-year campaign (2010-2012) to "transform" Falun Gong adherents, calling upon local governments, Party organizations, businesses, and individuals to step up efforts to reeducate practitioners and persuade or compel them to renounce their beliefs.[66]

According to the Dui Hua Foundation, Falun Gong adherents and other "cult" followers constitute an estimated two-thirds of all prisoners and detainees of conscience in China, or over 15,000 people.[67] Estimates of the number of Falun Gong practitioners who died in custody have ranged from several hundred to a few thousand. Falun Gong groups claim to have documented nearly 3,500 deaths in custody between 1999 and 2012, and they assert that the number of undocumented cases could be much higher.[68] Some groups allege that tens of thousands of Falun Gong prisoners were victims of illegal, non-consensual organ harvesting. Allegations of large-scale organ harvesting have not been independently verified.[69]

Gao Zhisheng

PRC authorities reportedly have harassed and detained lawyers who attempted to defend Falun Gong practitioners. Gao Zhisheng, a prominent rights lawyer who advocated for those whose homes or land had been seized by developers without fair compensation as well as for Falun Gong adherents, has been detained on and off since 2006. In late 2011, Gao reportedly began serving a three-year prison term that was handed down in 2006, but suspended for five years. During his periods of detention, security personnel allegedly have tortured Gao, denied him access to legal counsel and regular visits from his family, and withheld information about his location. Family members reportedly visited Gao in March 2012 and January 2013 at a prison in China's far western Xinjiang region. Government authorities reportedly warned them not to speak publicly about Gao or his condition.[70]

China's Family Planning Policies

China's "One-Child Policy," launched in 1980 to curb population growth, promotes an ideal of one child per family. Each province has its own family planning guidelines. Many jurisdictions allow for more than one child for ethnic minorities, rural couples in which the first child is a girl, couples in which both parents are only children, and in various other circumstances. China's 2002 Population and Family Planning Law does not explicitly condone abortion as a means of dealing with violations of the One-Child Policy, stating that "Family planning shall be practiced chiefly by means of contraception."[71] However, the national law does authorize other penalties for violators of the policy, including heavy fines and job-related sanctions, as well as the denial of public health and education benefits to offspring beyond the first child. The policy has led to many human rights abuses by local level officials attempting to enforce the law, including forced contraception, sterilization, and abortion. According to the CECC, in the past year, "authorities in a wide range of localities implemented population planning enforcement campaigns that employed coercive measures to prevent or terminate 'out-of plan' pregnancies."[72]

Although the central government has not proposed any fundamental changes to the One-Child Policy, it has tolerated a growing, public clamor for reform, particularly from Chinese demographic experts. Chinese family planning rules have contributed to not only sharply lower fertility rates, but also to an accelerated aging of the population and added strains on the social welfare system. Furthermore, the policy, along with a historical preference for boys based upon cultural and economic factors, has spurred the illegal but widespread practice of sex-selective abortions, particularly in rural areas, and resulted in a skewed gender ratio nationally. Chinese census data show that in 2011, 118 baby boys were born for every 100 baby girls, down from a peak of 121 boy babies for every 100 girl babies in 2008, but well above the normal global range of 103 to 107 boys per 100 girls.[73] In 2012, a Chinese government-affiliated think tank recommended that the government immediately relax the One-Child Policy, urging it to allow two children per family in some provinces by 2015 and to drop all birth limits by 2020.[74] Some analysts believe that the policy will likely be adjusted to allow most Chinese two children per household in the near future.[75] A 2012 case in China's Shaanxi Province, in which government officials forced a 22-year-old mother, Feng Jianmei, to undergo an abortion of her seven-monthold female fetus, renewed debate in China about family planning policies. The case came to light when the mother's outraged family posted photographs on the Internet of her in her hospital bed with her dead fetus by her side.[76]

Labor Issues

Labor unrest in China reflects a changing relationship between workers, enterprises, and the government. Wage pressures—caused by economic development, a shortage of young workers due to demographic changes, the rising value of China's currency, the *renminbi*, and greater enforcement of the 2008 Labor Contract Law—coupled with widening income disparities, a growing awareness of rights, and rising expectations among China's new generation of workers, have helped to fuel the unrest. In 2010, China experienced a surge in labor disputes, including three dozen strikes at Foxconn, Honda, Hyundai, and other foreign-owned factories in Guangdong province, one of China's principal manufacturing regions. In addition, many less-noticed labor incidents occurred "everywhere" and in "all kinds of enterprises."[77] At Taiwan electronics giant Foxconn, reportedly China's largest private employer and known as the world's largest supplier of components for global brands such as Apple, Microsoft, and Hewlett-Packard, strikes in some of its factories in China were preceded by the suicides of 11 Chinese employees earlier in the year. Many observers and labor activists attributed the suicides to highly demanding and stressful working conditions.[78]

Most labor protesters sought higher wages, improved working conditions, and enforcement of PRC labor laws, including limits on overtime, although some workers also demanded the right to elect their own union representatives or form their own unions. Some Chinese labor experts and officials expressed support for a greater advocacy role for China's official union, the All-China Federation of Trade Unions (ACFTU), and the process of collective bargaining. Some legislative proposals at the provincial and national levels supported the right to strike.[79]

Compared to past labor movements in China, the strikes of 2010 were unusual for several reasons: the official media covered them; they resulted in positive results for many workers, such as substantial pay raises; labor organizers skillfully used Internet social networking tools; and, in some cases, management negotiated directly with strike leaders.[80] However, as in the past, the activism of workers did not represent a national labor or political movement. For the most part, workers did not organize on a long-term basis or build linkages between enterprises, and their aims were narrow or focused on wages and working conditions. China's leaders, meanwhile, remained vigilant against the development of a national labor movement and continued to forbid the formation of independent unions.

Labor protests continued in 2011 and 2012, and one labor rights advocate reportedly died while in custody. In March 2012, the Washington, DC-based Fair Labor Association (FLA) documented poor working conditions at three factories owned by Foxconn. Foxconn and Apple agreed to take remedial measures, allow ongoing assessments by the FLA, and "ensure elections of worker representatives without management interference."[81] In 2012, new national laws governing labor dispute resolution went into effect, which may provide more ways for workers to present their grievances. Authorities in Guangdong province instituted secret ballot elections for trade union representatives in some factories in Shenzhen, but also harassed some labor NGOs, including destroying or cutting utilities to their offices or preventing them from renting spaces. Roughly 10 labor NGOs in Shenzhen were forced to close, ostensibly because they did not meet proper registration requirements.[82]

Other labor NGOs were encouraged to join a government-organized Federation of Social Service Organizations for Guangdong Workers, which is affiliated with the Guangdong ACFTU.[83] Nationally, little progress has been made in the areas of collective bargaining and the right to strike.

CIVIL SOCIETY

Chinese non-state entities play a small but growing role in social welfare, policy-making, and political discourse, although many of them rely upon the state for their economic or political survival. In 2012, the PRC government acknowledged the importance of civil society while attempting to harness its capabilities for its own ends, according to some observers. Some experts argue that this approach broadens the space for civil society while assuming a government role in shaping it. An editorial in the official *Global Times* opined that civil society plays a significant role in addressing and diluting social conflicts. Another commentary upheld Chinese NGOs as important partners in the government's social management and "social innovation" efforts.[84] In other cases, civil society actors have pushed the boundaries of permissible social activity at great personal risk. Lawyers, journalists, and activists have been at the forefront in helping to protect and promote human rights and the public interest, although many of them have faced government harassment and deprivation of their freedoms.

Social Organizations

Non-governmental organizations have become important players in Chinese society. Environmental groups have been at the forefront of the development of the NGO sector in China. Other areas in which non-state organizations operate include legal aid, public health, education, rural development, poverty alleviation, charity/philanthropy, and policy research. In the past year, some NGOs reportedly put forward legislative proposals to the National People's Congress and Chinese People's Political Consultative Conference, a government advisory body.[85]

Although in recent years PRC leaders have expressed an appreciation for the public contributions of NGOs (also known as social or civil society organizations),[86] they also have conveyed a wariness about their potential autonomy, intentions, and foreign contacts. In the middle of the last decade, after allowing nearly a decade of steady growth, Beijing began to tighten restrictions on social organizations. The government is especially fearful of the potential for Chinese civil society, in partnership with foreign NGOs, to help foment political unrest. Some PRC officials in charge of China's civil society organizations have complained that excessive constraints on the NGO sector have stifled its growth unnecessarily.[87]

Many Chinese social or civil society organizations face daunting and complicated challenges related to their legality, financing, and political survival. Social organizations are required to register with an official or quasi-official sponsor, such as a state agency or educational institution. Many groups experience difficulties finding an official organization willing to accept them or meeting financial requirements. Unregistered social organizations are more vulnerable to arbitrary government policies, including closure, and are not eligible for tax exemptions. Some civil society groups that cannot secure a sponsor choose to register as businesses. Some PRC sources indicate that China has over 460,000 registered social organizations, compared to 244,000 a decade ago. According to one estimate, 3 million to 4 million groups operate without official status.[88]

In 2012, requirements for NGOs to gain legal status were simplified in some major cities and regions. In various pilot programs, most types of social organizations were no longer required to find an official sponsor, and were allowed to apply directly with the local Civil Affairs Department. In some cities, a registered social organization would be regarded as "an independent legal entity responsible for its own behavior."[89] However, as mentioned above, Guangdong province, which leads the nation in NGO sector reforms, reportedly shut down a number of civil society organizations dedicated to migrant workers. Some observers believe this move reflected the provincial government's fear of labor unrest, despite its professed embrace of NGOs.[90]

THE INTERNET AND OTHER MEDIA DEVELOPMENTS

China has the world's largest number of Internet users, estimated at 564 million people, including an estimated 309 million people with accounts on Twitter-like microblogging sites.[91] China also has one of the most thorough and aggressive Internet censorship systems in the world. Human rights organizations report that 78 Chinese citizens are serving prison sentences for writing about politically sensitive topics online and 32 journalists are serving jail terms. The PRC has among the lowest levels of Internet and "new media" freedom in the world and is one of the lowest ranked countries for press freedom.[92]

Despite government efforts to limit the flow, Chinese Internet users are able to access unprecedented amounts of information. The web has served as a lifeline for political dissidents, social activists, and civil society actors. "Netizens" have helped to curb some abuses of government authority and compelled some officials to conduct affairs more openly.[93] The web also has enabled the public to occasionally engage in civil discourse on a national level. In the short space of three years, microblog sites (*weibo*), similar to Twitter, have become the most important source of news, "most prominent place for free speech," and the country's "most important public sphere."[94] Although Twitter is blocked in China, many Chinese, particularly those with international connections, find ways to access the service. Dissident artist Ai Weiwei continues to be an avid user of Twitter, despite efforts by state authorities to silence him. Both *weibo* and Twitter helped to keep Chinese supporters and foreign reporters apprised of Chen Guangcheng's status during the diplomatic standoff over his fate. The state has the capability to block news of events and to partially shut down the Internet. As noted above, in Xinjiang, the government blocked the Internet for 10 months following the ethnic unrest in 2009. Nonetheless, politically sensitive news often gets disseminated, if only fleetingly, due to the sheer volume of information on the Internet.[95]

The PRC government employs a variety of methods to control online content and expression. These include website or IP address blocking and keyword filtering by routers at the country's eight Internet "gateways," telecommunications company data centers, and Internet portals; regulating and monitoring Internet service providers, Internet cafes, and university bulletin board systems; and occasional arrests of high-profile "cyber dissidents." To comply with government directives, large Internet portals and blogging services are estimated to each employ hundreds of people to filter online discussion.[96] In May 2011, the PRC government created a new central body, the State Internet Information Office, to better coordinate the myriad agencies that oversee the Internet in China.

Blocked websites, social networking sites, and file sharing sites include Radio Free Asia, Voice of America (Chinese language), international human rights websites, many Taiwanese news sites, Facebook, Twitter, and YouTube. Online English language news sites, including the Voice of America, the *New York Times*, and the *Washington Post*, are generally accessible or only occasionally or selectively censored. Commonly barred Internet searches and microblog postings include those with direct and indirect or disguised references to Tibet; the Tiananmen suppression of 1989; Falun Gong; PRC leaders and dissidents who have been involved in recent, politically sensitive events, scandals, or issues; democracy; highly charged foreign affairs issues; and sexual material. The government reportedly also has hired thousands of students and other Internet commentators to express pro-government views on websites, bulletin boards, and chat rooms.[97]

For Chinese Internet users in search of blocked information from outside the PRC's Internet gateways, or "Great Firewall," circumventing government controls (also known as *fanqiang* or "scaling the wall") is made possible by downloading special software. These methods mainly include proxy servers, which are free but somewhat cumbersome, and virtual private networks (VPNs), which are available at a cost (roughly $40.00), but also enable secure communication.[98] Proxy servers and VPNs enable some motivated Internet users to avoid censorship, but impose just enough inconvenience to keep foreign information out of the reach of most Chinese users. The use of these tools is often tolerated by the government as long as it remains politically manageable, according to some observers.

In addition to the effectiveness of censorship, some studies show that the vast majority of Internet users in China do not engage the medium for political purposes. Although a small community of dissidents and activists use the web to broach political topics, they reportedly make up a small minority—less than 10% of all users according to some estimates. Between 1% and 8% of web users in China access proxy servers and virtual private networks to get around government-erected Internet firewalls to access censored content—both political and non-political. Moreover, many Chinese reportedly accept the government's justification that it regulates the Internet in order to control illegal, harmful, or dangerous online content, services, and activities, such as pornography, gambling, slander, cyberattacks, and social networking by criminal organizations.[99]

Since Internet use became widespread in China in the mid-2000s, the government and Chinese netizens have engaged in a game of cat and mouse, with new communications technologies and services and novel censorship circumvention methods challenging the government's efforts to control the web, followed by crackdowns or new regulations, and then a repeat of the cycle. In the latest round of the struggle, in December 2012, the government enacted a new law requiring those who apply for an Internet or mobile service account to use their real names. Related legislation calls for service providers to delete posts that are deemed illegal. Beijing reportedly also has increased interference with circumvention tools used by many web users to surmount the Great Firewall.[100]

The new measures have raised anger and concern among both netizens and Internet companies. Some Internet users have proclaimed that the requirements reduce the space for free expression. Sina Weibo, which offers a Twitter-like microblogging service, reportedly has resisted past government pressures to register real names. The company reportedly expressed alarm about the new laws, suggesting that they will result in service disruptions and the decline of its user base.[101] The government claims that these measures are part of its efforts to improve web security, including protecting Internet users' personal information, reducing online rumors and harassment, preventing libel, cracking down on spam e-mail, and combating pornography. An opinion piece published by the government news agency argued that the new laws would not restrict freedom of speech nor hamper the use of the Internet to expose official corruption.[102]

Protests for Press Freedom

In January 2013, journalists, press freedom advocates, and citizens across the country took to *weibo* to protest government actions at two newspapers—the reform-minded *Southern Weekly* and the *Beijing News*. The Guangzhou-based *Southern Weekly's* editors planned to publish a commentary in support of constitutional government, which was replaced, some Chinese journalists say, by a tribute to the Communist Party written by the provincial propaganda chief. The interference by higher authorities reportedly triggered a strike by staff at the newspaper and demonstrations in front of its headquarters, although the protest was quelled in time for the next issue of the paper to come out on time.

The *Beijing News* publisher, Dai Zigeng, reportedly threatened to resign rather than print the government's version of these events, which blamed the conflict at the *Southern Weekly* on "hostile foreign forces." Some experts opined that the protests were a unique example of both journalists and ordinary people expressing support for free speech, and that more protests were likely in the future.[103]

HUMAN RIGHTS REFORMS/LEGISLATION

During the past several years, the PRC government has enacted some laws aimed at reducing some of the most serious patterns of human rights abuse. New measures designed to protect or promote human rights include those related to criminal defendants, the use of torture, organ transplants, the death penalty, labor conditions, and private property. The lack of transparency, enforcement, and oversight mechanisms prevent many legal protections from having a significant impact. However, the reforms may provide some basis for citizens to claim their rights under the law. Major laws related to rights protections include the following:

- **Criminal Procedure Law:** Amendments to the Criminal Procedure Law, which went into effect in January 2013, provide for greater protections against torture and coerced confessions, expanded access to legal defense, longer trial deliberations, mandatory appellate hearings, more rigorous judicial review, and greater government oversight of the legal process. Other changes in the law are designed to improve the treatment of juveniles, women, and people on death row. However, the revised law also sanctions the use of "residential surveillance" or secret detention centers (for up to six months) for suspects in cases involving state security. Many analysts argue that this practice leaves detainees, particularly political dissidents, highly vulnerable to arbitrary treatment and abuse by security personnel.[104]
- **Organ Transplants:** In 2007, the Ministry of Health implemented regulations requiring written consent from organ donors, banning the sale of human organs, restricting organ donors mainly to family members of those needing transplants, and limiting the number of hospitals performing transplants. In 2011, the PRC Criminal Law was revised to include organ trafficking as a crime. In 2012, the government announced its intention to end the illegal trade in organs and to phase out the transplantation of organs from executed prisoners within five years.[105] These restrictions followed international criticism of an allegedly booming, unregulated international trade in organs of executed Chinese prisoners.
- **The Death Penalty:** The number of executions in China has declined, to around 3,000 per year, according to some estimates.[106] In 2010, the National People's Congress amended the Criminal Law to reduce the

number of crimes punishable by death from 68 to 55. In May 2011, the Supreme People's Court instructed lower courts to suspend death sentences for two years for "all cases that do not require immediate execution."[107]

- **State Secrets Law:** In 2010, the PRC government amended the Law on Guarding State Secrets. The changes, while tightening government control over the Internet, also reduced the scope of the law, clarified its terms, and promised greater transparency. Some observers hoped that the amendments would reduce the number of prosecutions of people accused of stealing or leaking state secrets. However, according to most experts, the law remains vague and still can be used broadly against political dissidents and others.[108]

- **State Compensation Law:** In 2010, the National People's Congress approved amendments to the State Compensation Law, which would grant citizens greater powers to obtain compensation when the state is found to have violated their rights or acted negligently.

- **Labor Rights:** The Labor Contract Law of 2008 provided for greater protections of the rights of workers and stronger enforcement of regulations related to working conditions. The law reportedly spurred a dramatic rise in labor dispute arbitration cases and strikes, and was a catalyst for the surge in labor unrest in 2010.

- **Property Rights:** In 2007, the National People's Congress passed a constitutional amendment designed to protect property rights that had been debated since 2002. The new property law aimed to protect private entrepreneurs, urban home owners, and farmers whose crop lands often risk seizure by government-backed real estate developers. In 2008, the government issued new measures allowing farmers to lease and sell rights to use the property allocated to them by the state.[109]

- **Government Transparency:** In 2007, the PRC government announced new rules requiring greater disclosure of official information.[110] In addition, institutional and legal mechanisms were established to provide for greater government responsiveness and accountability. In part, these measures represented attempts to compel local governments to reveal financial accounts related to land takings in rural areas.[111]

U.S. EFFORTS TO ADVANCE HUMAN RIGHTS IN CHINA

Many experts and policy makers have sharply disagreed over the best policy approaches and methods to apply toward human rights issues in China. Differing U.S. goals include promoting fundamental political change in the PRC and supporting incremental progress. A perennial challenge is how to balance U.S. values against sometimes incompatible U.S. interests in the relationship. Possible approaches range from placing human rights conditions upon bilateral ties to inducing democratic change through bilateral and international engagement.

Since the end of the 1980s, successive U.S. administrations have employed broadly similar strategies for promoting human rights in China. Some analysts have referred to the U.S. foreign policy approach of promoting democracy in China through diplomatic and economic engagement, without directly challenging Communist Party rule, as a strategy of "peaceful evolution."[112] President Bill Clinton referred to this policy as "constructive engagement"—furthering diplomatic and economic ties while pressing for open markets and democracy, calling it "our best hope to secure our own interest and values and to advance China's."[113] President George W. Bush also came to view U.S. engagement as the most effective means of promoting U.S. interests and freedom in China.[114] As China's importance in global economic, security, environmental, and other matters has grown, the Obama Administration, like the Bush Administration, has attempted to forge bilateral cooperation on many fronts, while disagreeing with Beijing on many human rights issues. In his remarks during the summit with PRC President Hu Jintao in January 2011, President Obama referred to the universality of the freedoms of speech, assembly, and religion, a point frequently made by President Clinton. Echoing a theme evoked by George W. Bush in his second term, Obama also suggested that greater respect for human rights in China would benefit China's success and global stability.[115]

Congressional Actions

The U.S. Congress has been at the forefront of U.S. human rights policy toward China, through such measures and efforts as sanctions, resolutions, hearings, and foreign assistance in support of human rights and democracy in China and in Tibetan areas of the PRC. Congress imposed sanctions following the Tiananmen military crackdown in 1989 and has withheld support for

United Nations Population Fund programs in China. Members of Congress have introduced resolutions calling attention to human rights abuses in the PRC, including the imprisonment and detention of political and religious figures; persecution of Tibetans, Uighurs, and Falun Gong adherents; censorship of the Internet and other mass media; coercive abortions; and the deportation of North Korean refugees. Foreign operations appropriations measures have authorized and funded democracy, human rights, rule of law, and Internet freedom programs in China and economic, cultural, and environmental programs in Tibet and Tibetan areas.

In recent years, the following committees have held hearings related to human rights in China: the House Committee on Foreign Affairs; the Africa, Global Health, Global Human Rights, and International Organizations and the Asia and the Pacific subcommittees of the House Committee on Foreign Affairs; and the Subcommittee on Immigration Policy and Enforcement of the House Committee on the Judiciary. Topics have included the Congressional-Executive Commission on China annual report; the China Democracy Promotion Act; the crackdown on dissent in 2011; the one-child policy; Internet censorship; Chinese rights defenders; the repatriation of North Korean refugees; labor conditions; and U.S. foreign assistance to China. The CECC, the Tom Lantos Human Rights Commission, the U.S. Commission on International Religious Freedom, and other congressional and congressionally mandated bodies and fora have also investigated, publicized, and reported on human rights conditions in China.

Selected Policy Tools

Many U.S. experts and policy makers have disagreed over the best methods to apply toward promoting democracy and human rights in China. The U.S. government has often employed a range of means simultaneously. Policy tools include sanctions; open criticism of PRC human rights policies; quiet diplomacy; international pressure; bilateral dialogue; foreign assistance programs; Internet freedom efforts; public diplomacy; and support of dissident and pro-democracy groups in China and the United States.

Sanctions
Many U.S. sanctions on the PRC in response to the Tiananmen military crackdown in 1989 remain in effect, including some foreign aid-related restrictions, such as required "no" votes or abstentions by U.S. representatives

in international financial institutions on loans to China (except those that meet basic human needs).[116] Since 2004, Congress has required that U.S. representatives to international financial institutions support projects in Tibet only if they do not encourage the migration and settlement of non-Tibetans into Tibet or the transfer of Tibetan-owned properties to non-Tibetans, which some policymakers fear may further erode Tibetan culture and identity.[117] Foreign operations appropriations measures have prohibited support to the United Nations Population Fund from being used for programs in China.[118]

Openly Criticizing China

Some analysts argue that the U.S. government should take principled stands against China's human rights abuses more openly, forcefully, and frequently, while other experts believe that more overt efforts can undermine human rights objectives. Many prominent Chinese dissidents have claimed that international pressure or attention protected them from harsher treatment by PRC authorities. Other observers suggest that open criticism of PRC human rights policies by the U.S. government can both hearten reform-minded Chinese and provoke hardliners in the PRC leadership or create greater suspicion of foreign influences and ties.

Principled Pragmatism

During the Obama Administration's first term, former Secretary of State Hillary Clinton described the Administration's human rights policy as one of "principled pragmatism." This notion is based upon the premise that tough but quiet diplomacy is both less disruptive to the overall relationship and more effective in producing change than public censure. Clinton's approach also may have played a role in the efforts by U.S. diplomats to secure the release of rights advocate Chen Guangcheng from Chinese authorities so that he could study law in the United States, while simultaneously participating in the bilateral Strategic and Economic Dialogue (S&ED) in May 2012.[119]

The Obama Administration has openly pressed China on human rights issues in a number of cases. During his visit to China in November 2009, President Obama briefly spoke about human rights and Internet freedom during a town hall meeting with university students in Shanghai. Although the broadcast of the speech was limited to Shanghai and transcripts on the Internet were censored, thousands of Chinese reportedly accessed the White House website and cheered Obama's appeal for Internet freedom.[120] Former Secretary Clinton spoke out on human rights issues, including criticizing China's Internet censorship and alleged hacking of U.S. companies in January 2010, demanding Nobel laureate Liu Xiaobo's release from prison in October 2010, calling for the freedom of dissident artist Ai Weiwei in April 2011, and discussing China's human rights record, calling it "deplorable," in a June 2011 interview.[121] Vice-President Joe Biden, on a trip to China in 2011 to meet then-PRC Vice-President Xi Jinping, told his Chinese hosts that "allowing for greater human rights would make China, like the U.S., more stable and strong, rather than harming its economic progress."[122]

In May 2012, at the conclusion of the S&ED in Beijing, former Secretary Clinton spoke on several key bilateral issues, including cooperation on addressing international issues such as the North Korean and Iranian nuclear programs, the civil war in Syria, and human rights in China. She stated, "We raise specific matters of individuals and situations whenever necessary because we cannot ignore our areas of difference in the comprehensive relationship that we are building." PRC State Councilor Dai Bingguo responded that "no country can claim to be perfect," and that human rights should not be used as an "excuse to interfere in the internal affairs of countries."[123]

United Nations Human Rights Council

The United Nations Human Rights Council was formed in 2006 to replace the U.N. Commission on Human Rights (UNCHR), which had been faulted for being unduly influenced by nondemocratic countries. The United States had sponsored several resolutions at the UNCHR criticizing China's human rights record, but none were successful; China was able to thwart voting on most resolutions through "no-action motions."[124] The PRC has often been able to employ its soft power—diplomatic and economic influence—in global fora in order to reduce international pressure to improve its human rights conditions. The Bush Administration opposed the formation of the Council and declined to become a member, arguing that it did not offer improvements over the UNCHR and that it would place too much focus on Israel. The Obama Administration sought and was granted a seat on the Human Rights Council in June 2009.[125]

The United Nations established the Universal Periodic Review (UPR) mechanism by which the Human Rights Council assesses the human rights records of all U.N. members once every four years. The UPR Working Group conducted a periodic review of China in February 2009.

Representatives of some countries voiced serious concerns about China's human rights record, while representatives of some developing and non-democratic countries expressed support of China.[126] China's next review is scheduled for October-November 2013. The PRC reportedly has not fulfilled several recommendations that it agreed to during its first review, including ratifying the International Covenant on Civil and Political Rights and accepting a visit by the U.N. Office of the High Commissioner for Human Rights. The United States, which was an observer but not yet a member of the Human Rights Council in February 2009, is expected to take a much more active and critical approach during China's next review.[127]

Human Rights Dialogue

The U.S.-China human rights dialogue was established in 1990. It is one of eight government-togovernment dialogues between China and other countries on human rights. Beijing formally suspended the process in 2004 after the Bush Administration sponsored an unsuccessful U.N. resolution criticizing China's human rights record. The talks were resumed in May 2008, after a gap of six years. The Obama Administration has participated in three rounds between 2010 and 2012, co-chaired by then U.S. Assistant Secretary of State for Democracy, Human Rights, and Labor Michael Posner and PRC Ministry of Foreign Affairs, Department of International Organizations Director General Chen Xu.

The 17th round of the dialogue took place in July 2012 in Washington, DC. The meetings also included a visit to the United States Supreme Court and U.S. nongovernmental and media organizations. U.S. officials brought up a number of individual cases, including those of Chinese dissidents, rights activists, lawyers, journalists, bloggers, NGO leaders, and religious figures. U.S. interlocutors reportedly raised the case of Chen Kegui, the nephew of Chen Guangcheng, and Feng Jianmei of Shaanxi Province, who had been detained and forced to have a late-term abortion. Other concerns included the persecution of Uighurs in Xinjiang and Chinese policies that may have contributed to the self-immolations in Tibet.[128]

Some experts have criticized the bilateral human rights dialogue for providing both governments with opportunities for claiming achievements on human rights issues in China, without establishing benchmarks for progress or imposing penalties for failing to produce results. They have expressed concern that separating the human rights dialogue from the S&ED has marginalized human rights issues, and that the dialogue lacks coordination with other U.S. agencies. Furthermore, they say, the human rights dialogue is not sufficiently transparent and does not include participation from other stakeholders, including Members of Congress, nongovernmental organizations, and human rights activists.[129]

Administration officials respond to critics by explaining that the human rights dialogue is an important means by which to regularly express U.S. positions on human rights, and not an arena for negotiation. U.S. participants aim to "amplify" the voices of Chinese citizens on human rights issues, and to discuss them in greater depth. U.S. officials contend that the human rights dialogue is one of many channels of communication on human rights and not intended to remove the topic of human rights from the S&ED. They argue that the talks enable the U.S. government to focus on human rights within one forum, and suggest that, given the deep disagreements on human rights and other contentious issues, the holding of the bilateral dialogue and the agreement to continue them represent positive steps.[130] Furthermore, some observers contend, the absence of the dialogue would undermine other U.S. efforts to promote human rights in China.

A related bilateral dialogue, the Legal Experts Dialogue (LED), was launched in 2003. The Obama Administration convened the fourth round in 2011, the first since 2005. The LED is designed to serve as a forum to discuss the means of implementing an effective system of law. At the April 2012 LED, the U.S. delegation was headed by Harold Koh, Legal Adviser of the Department of State, and Assistant Secretary Michael Posner. The PRC side included members of the Supreme People's Court and National People's Congress, officials from the Ministry of Justice, Ministry of Public Security, and Supreme People's Procuratorate, and representatives of the Chinese Academy of Social Sciences and the All China Lawyers' Association. The four main agenda items were community corrections, the role of lawyers, legal aid, and counterterrorism and human rights.[131]

Rule of Law and Civil Society Programs

Since 2001, foreign operations appropriations measures have funded democracy and human rights programs in China. Between 2001 and 2012, the United States government authorized or made available $338 million for Department of State and U.S. Agency for International Development (USAID) foreign assistance efforts in the PRC, including Peace Corps programs. Of this amount, $279 million was devoted to democracy, human rights, rule of law, and related activities; Tibetan communities; and the environment. Program activities have included developing democratic norms and institutions; training legal professionals; building the capacity of judicial institutions; reforming the criminal justice system; and supporting sustainable livelihoods and cultural preservation in Tibetan communities. The direct recipients of State Department and USAID grants have been predominantly U.S.-based non-governmental organizations and universities. Some Chinese NGOs, universities, and government entities have participated in, collaborated with, or indirectly benefited from U.S. programs and foreign aid grantees. Appropriations for Department of State and USAID programs in China reached a peak in FY2010, totaling $46.9 million. Funding decreased by nearly 40% between 2010 and 2012, resulting in the discontinuation of a number of rule of law and environmental programs.[134]

Congressional-Executive Commission on China

Between 1989 and 1999, the U.S. Congress sought to monitor and hold the PRC government accountable for human rights violations through the annual renewal of "most favored nation" (MFN) trading status. In 2000, the legislation that granted permanent normal trade relations (PNTR) treatment to China (P.L. 106-286), ended this mechanism, but included provisions on human rights. The PNTR Act created the Congressional-Executive Commission on China (CECC) to monitor human rights and the rule of law in China and to submit an annual report with recommendations to the President and Congress.[132] Title III of the act provides that the Commission shall consist of nine Senators, nine Members of the House of Representatives, five senior Administration officials appointed by the President, and a staff of 10. The Commission holds hearings and roundtables on rights-related topics, provides related news and analysis, keeps track of pertinent PRC laws and regulations, and maintains a database of political prisoners. The CECC has an annual operating budget of approximately $2 million.[133]

Internet Freedom

The U.S. government has undertaken efforts to promote global Internet freedom. In 2006, the Bush Administration established the Global Internet Freedom Task Force (GIFT). Continued under the Obama Administration as the NetFreedom Task Force, the grouping's duties are to coordinate policy within the State Department on Internet freedom efforts, monitor Internet freedom around the world, respond to challenges to Internet freedom, and expand global access to the Internet. Congress appropriated $50 million for U.S. government global Internet freedom efforts between FY2008 and FY2010, $20 million in FY2011, and $25 million in FY2012. Program areas include censorship circumvention technology, Internet and mobile communications security training, media and advocacy skills, and public policy. The primary target countries of such efforts, particularly circumvention and secure communications programs, have been China and Iran.

U.S. congressional committees and commissions have held hearings on the Internet and China, including the roles of U.S. Internet companies in China's censorship regime, cyber security, free trade in Internet services, and intellectual property rights. The Global Internet Freedom Caucuses, founded in 2010 and currently chaired in the House by Representative Chris Smith and in the Senate by Senators Chris Coons, Mark Kirk, and Bob Casey, Jr., aim to promote online freedom of information and expression. The Global Online Freedom Act (GOFA), first introduced in 2006, has evolved through four Congresses. The most recent version of the bill in the 113th Congress, The Global Online Freedom Act of 2013 (H.R. 491), aims to "prevent United States businesses from cooperating with repressive governments in transforming the Internet into a tool of censorship and surveillance, to fulfill the responsibility of the United States Government to promote freedom of expression on the Internet...."[135]

Public Diplomacy

U.S. public diplomacy programs aim to expose Chinese participants, many of them young and/or educated, to U.S. politics, society, culture, and academia; sponsor exchanges; and promote mutual understanding. According to the Department of State, approximately one-third of all Chinese citizens participating in U.S.-sponsored professional exchange programs work in fields related to democracy, rights, and religion.[136] In 2011, 733 U.S. citizens and 959 PRC citizens participated in exchange programs sponsored by the State Department's Bureau of Educational and Cultural Affairs.[137]

International Broadcasting

The Voice of America (VOA) and Radio Free Asia (RFA) provide external sources of independent or alternative news and opinion to Chinese audiences. The two media services play small but unique roles in providing tastes of U.S.-style broadcasting, journalism, and public debate in China. VOA, which offers mainly U.S. and international news, and RFA, which serves as an uncensored source of domestic Chinese news, often report on critical world and local events to Chinese audiences. The PRC government regularly jams and blocks VOA and RFA Mandarin, Cantonese, Tibetan, and Uighur language broadcasts and Internet sites, while VOA English services receive less interference. Both VOA and RFA are making efforts to upgrade their Internet services and circumvention or counter-censorship technologies.

VOA "Special English" international news programs, aimed at intermediate learners of English, are popular with many young, educated, and professional Chinese.

National Endowment for Democracy

Established by the U.S. government in 1983 to promote freedom around the world, the National Endowment for Democracy (NED) is a private, non-profit organization that receives an annual appropriation from Congress. NED has played a major role in promoting democracy in China since the mid-1980s. Activities of NED and its core institutes include supporting Chinese pro-democracy organizations in the United States and Hong Kong, helping to advance the rule of law in China, promoting the rights of workers and women in the PRC, and assisting the development of Tibetan communities. The Endowment's China programs have received support through the annual foreign operations appropriation for NED (an estimated $118 million in FY2012) and congressional earmarks to NED for democracy-related programs in the PRC and in Tibet. In addition, the Department of State has provided direct grants to NED's core institutes.[138]

End Notes

[1] See David M. Lampton, "'The China Fantasy,' Fantasy," *The China Quarterly*, No. 191 (September 2007); James Mann, "Rejoinder to David M. Lampton," *The China Quarterly*, No. 191 (September 2007); "Not So Obvious: The Secretary of State Underestimates the Power of Her Words," *Washington Post*, February 2009; "A Bow to Reality, Not China," *USA Today*, February 27, 2009; Thomas J. Christensen, "Shaping the Choices of a Rising China: Recent Lessons for the Obama Administration," *The Washington Quarterly*, July 2009; William F. Schulz, "Strategic Persistence: How the United States Can Help Improve Human Rights in China," *Center for American Progress*, January 2009.

[2] For example, see Robert P. Weller, "Responsive Authoritarianism," in Bruce Gilley and Larry Diamond, eds., *Political Change in China: Comparisons with Taiwan*, Boulder: Lynne Reinner Publishers, 2008.

[3] Linda Yeung, "Reform School," *South China Morning Post*, November 28, 2010.

[4] Sophie Richardson, "Let a Hundred Volunteers Bloom," *Foreign Affairs*, October 11, 2012.

[5] Jie Chen, "Attitudes toward Democracy and the Behavior of China's Middle Class," in Cheng Li, ed. *China's Emerging Middle Class*, Washington: Brookings Institution Press, 2010.

[6] "Growing Concerns in China about Inequality, Corruption," *Pew Research Center Global Attitudes Project*, October 16, 2012.

[7] "Changes and Challenges for China in 2013," *Council on Foreign Relations*, December 26, 2012; Cary Huang, "'Reform or Perish,' Journal Warns Communist Party," *South China Morning Post*, October 19, 2012.

[8] Shi Jiangtao, "Mainland Scholars Petition Communist Party for Change," *South China Morning Post*, December 27, 2012; Verna Yu, "China Petition Urges Rights Reforms," *South China Morning Post*, February 27, 2013.

[9] Former Premier Wen Jiabao expressed support for expanding direct elections for executive positions to the country and township levels, as part of a gradual process. Keith Richburg, "China's Premier Again Calls for Political Reform," *Washington Post*, March 14, 2011; Ministry of Foreign Affairs of the People's Republic of China, "Premier Wen Jiabao Meets the Press," March 15, 2012.

[10] Sui-Lee Wee, "China Village Ends Protests after Government Compromise," *Reuters*, December 21, 2011; Tom Orlik, "Unrest Grows as Economy Booms," *Wall Street Journal*, September 26, 2011. The PRC government no longer issues official statistics on mass incidents.

[11] Nicholas Bequelin, "Does the Law Matter in China?" *International Herald Tribune*, May 14, 2012.

[12] Congressional-Executive Commission on China, *Annual Report 2012*, October 10, 2012.

[13] Henry Sanderson and Michael Forsythe, "China Boosts Defense Spending as Military Modernizes Arsenal," *Bloomberg News*, March 5, 2013.

[14] "China Activists Die in Custody During Stability Sweep," *Agence France-Presse*, November 19, 2012.

[15] Wang, a contender for a position on the Standing Committee of the Political Bureau, was not selected at the Party Congress in 2012, thus disappointing many of his supporters.

[16] "Wukan Claims Success as First Election Ends," *Agence France-Presse*, March 5, 2012; "'Opportunity for Democracy': Rebel Chinese Village Votes" *Reuters*, March 3, 2012.

[17] Brian Fung, "Wukan Revisited: No, China's Village Experiment in Democracy Isn't Over," *The Atlantic*, September 23, 2012.

[18] Yizhen Zheng, "Carrying Out Grassroots Democracy in China: Two Local Experiments in Governance," China Elections and Governance (The Carter Center), March 3, 2011; Keith B. Richburg, "More Independents Running in China," *Washington Post*, September 10, 2011; Congressional—Executive Commission on China, op. cit. For further information, see CRS Report R41007, *Understanding China's Political System*, by Susan V. Lawrence and Michael F. Martin.

[19] For further information, see CRS Report R42554, *U.S.-China Diplomacy Over Chinese Legal Advocate Chen Guangcheng*, by Susan V. Lawrence and Thomas Lum.

[20] "Prominent Chinese Activist Blasts Nephew's Conviction," *CNN*, December 1, 2012.

[21] "Two Tibetans Die in Burning Protests," *Radio Free Asia*, April 25, 2013; "Dalai Lama Cautions Against Self-Immolations," *South China Morning Post*, June 14, 2013.

[22] "Burning in Tibet," *The Toronto Sun*, December 16, 2012; "China Outlines Criminal Punishments for Tibetan Self-Immolations," Dui Hua Foundation, December 5, 2012; "China Arrests Five Tibetans for 'Inciting' Immolation," *Associated Press*, February 28, 2013.

[23] U.S. Department of State, Statement by the Special Coordinator for Tibetan Issues Maria Otero, December 5, 2012.

[24] For more complete descriptions of human rights abuses, see Congressional-Executive Commission on China, *Annual Report 2012*, October 10, 2012, and Department of State, *Country Reports on Human Rights Practices for 2012 (China)*, April 19, 2013.

[25] Dui Hua Foundation, January 2013. Dui Hua Foundation experts caution that it is difficult to determine how many political and religious prisoners there are in China due to limited data and varied definitions.

[26] "Chinese State Security Arrests Stay High, Trials Soar," *Dui Hua Foundation*, November 19, 2012.

[27] U.S. Department of State, *2009 Human Rights Report: China*, March 11, 2010; Falun Gong organizations have placed the number as far higher.

[28] Maya Wang, "Rights Group: China May Not Be Ready for Labor Camp Reforms," *CNN*, January 16, 2013; Minnie Chan, "Kinder Face for Notorious Re-education Camps," *South China Morning Post*, February 21, 2007; Jim Yardley, "Issue in China: Many Jails without Trial," *New York Times*, May 9, 2005.

[29] Dui Hua Foundation, January 2013.

[30] Tang was released after the story broke. Dui Hua Foundation, "Consensus Building on RTL Reform, Cases Highlight Abuse," September 24, 2012; Zhang Pinghui, "Projects Hint at Reform of Mainland's Re-education Through Labor Policy," *South China Morning Post*, September 4, 2012.

[31] "Yunnan Stops Some Terms of 'Re-education Through Labour' Camps," *Agence France-Presse*, February 7, 2013.

[32] William Wan, "In China, Labor Camps Face an Uncertain Future," *Washington Post*, March 4, 2013.

[33] "China: Fully Abolish Re-education Through Labor," *Human Rights Watch Asia*, January 8, 2013.

[34] Ami Li, "Beijing Black Jail 'Releases Thousands of Petitioners'," *South China Morning Post*, December 5, 2012.

[35] Peter Ford, "Is China Cleaning Up Its Illegal 'Black Jails'?" *Christian Science Monitor*, February 4, 2013.

[36] "Charter '08" was inspired by "Charter 77," the Czechoslovakian democratic movement.

[37] Dui Hua Foundation, *Prisoner Update*, February 28, 2013.

[38] Dui Hua Foundation, *Prisoner Update*, June 3, 2013.

[39] Elizabeth Lynch, "I Pledge Allegiance to the CCP...," *China Law and Policy*, March 22, 2012.

[40] Department of State, *Country Reports on Human Rights Practices for 2011*, May 2012.

[41] "'Big Stick 306' and China's Contempt for the Law," *New York Times*, May 5, 2011.

[42] See United States Commission on International Religious Freedom, http://www.uscirf.gov/reports-and-briefs/annualreport.html; "China: Should Religious Freedom Be a "Core Interest"? *Forum 18 News Service*, February 7, 2013; Office of the Spokesperson, "Ambassador at Large for International Religious Freedom Visits China," April 30, 2013.

[43] Pew Research Center, Pew Forum on Religious and Public Life, 2012.

[44] "Three Self" refers to self-governance, self-support, and self-propagation, or independence from foreign missionary and other religious groups and influences.

[45] "2012's Top 10 Cases of Persecution of Churches and Christians in China," *China Aid Association*, January 16, 2013.

[46] Congressional-Executive Commission on China, op. cit.

[47] ChinaAid Association, *2011 Annual Report: Chinese Government Persecution of Christians and Churches in Mainland China*, February 2012.

[48] Portions of this section were written by Susan Lawrence, Specialist in Asian Affairs.

[49] "'Benefit the Masses' Campaign Surveilling Tibetans," *Human Rights Watch Asia*, June 19, 2013.

[50] Department of State, *Country Reports on Human Rights Practices for 2011*, op. cit.

[51] Congressional-Executive Commission on China, op. cit.

[52] "Tibet's Population Tops 3 Million; 90% Are Tibetans," *Xinhua*, May 4, 2011.

[53] "Han Chinese Migrants Killing Tibet's Way of Life," *The Tibet Post International*, July 26, 2010.

[54] Central Tibetan Administration, *NBC Interviews His Holiness the Dalai Lama on Self-immolation Tragedy in Tibet*, October 22, 2013, http://tibet.net/2012/10/23/nbc-interviews-his-holiness-the-dalai-lama-on-self-immolation-tragedyin-tibet/; "Dalai Lama Cautions Against Self-Immolations," op. cit.

[55] "Lodi Gyari: No Progress in Sino-Tibet Dialogue under Hu Jintao," *Phayul.com*, January 1, 2013.

[56] For further information, see CRS Report R41108, *U.S.-China Relations: Policy Issues*, by Susan V. Lawrence.

[57] Many Uighur exile groups prefer the name East Turkestan rather than the Chinese name of Xinjiang.

[58] Preeti Bhattacharji, "Uighurs and China's Xinjiang Region," *Council on Foreign Relations Backgrounder*, July 6, 2009.

[59] ETIM is on the United States' and United Nations' lists of terrorist organizations.

[60] Congressional-Executive Commission on China, op. cit.

[61] Ishaan Tharoor, "Tearing Down Old Kashgar: Another Blow to the Uighurs," *Time*, Wednesday, July 29, 2009.

[62] Alim Abdureyim and Ablikim Abdureyim were sentenced by a Xinjiang court in 2006 and 2007 to seven and nine years in prison, respectively.

[63] "Xinjiang Violence Leaves 21 Dead," *Radio Free Asia*, April 24, 2013; "China Urges U.S., After Boston Bombings, to Condemn Xinjiang 'Terrorism'," *Reuters*, April 25, 2013; "China Arrests 19 'Terrorists' Linked to Xinjiang Violence," *Voice of America*, April 30, 2013; "China Says No Foreign Link in Xinjiang Violence," *Associated Press*, May 2, 2013.

[64] Li Hongzhi is believed to live in the United States.

[65] James W. Tong, Prepared Statement, "Falun Gong in China: Review and Update," Congressional-Executive Commission on China, Roundtable, December 18, 2012.

[66] "Communist Party Calls for Increased Efforts to 'Transform' Falun Gong Practitioners as Part of Three-Year Campaign," Congressional-Executive Commission on China, March 22, 2011.

[67] Dui Hua Foundation, January 2013.

[68] See Falun Dafa Information Center, http://www.faluninfo.net/.

[69] The principal sources supporting the allegations of large-scale organ harvesting of Falun Gong prisoners include the following: David Matas and David Kilgour, *Report into Allegations of Organ Harvesting of Falun Gong Practitioners in China*, July 6, 2006; David Matas and David Kilgour, *Revised Report into Allegations of Organ Harvesting of Falun Gong Practitioners in China*, January 31, 2007; Ethan Gutmann, "China's Gruesome Organ Harvest," *The Weekly Standard*, November 11, 2008; David Matas and David Kilgour, *Bloody Harvest*, Woodstock (ON): Seraphim Editions, 2009; Davis Matas and Dr. Torsten Trey, eds., *State Organs: Transplant Abuse in China*, Woodstock (ON): Seraphim Editions, 2012.

[70] Edward Wong, "Family's Visit Pierces Silence on Jailed Chinese Dissident," *New York Times*, January 24, 2013.

[71] Population and Family Planning Law of the People's Republic of China (Order of the President No.63), Chapter III, Article 19, http://english.gov.cn/laws

[72] Congressional-Executive Commission on China, op. cit.

[73] "China's Gender Imbalance Still Grave," *Xinhua News Agency* via *China Daily*, March 29, 2012.

[74] "Chinese Government Think Tank Urges End to One-Child Policy," *Associated Press*, October 31, 2012.

[75] "China's One-Child Policy May Be Coming to an End," *Reuters*, January 22, 2013.

[76] David Barboza, "China Suspends Family Planning Workers after Forced Abortion," *New York Times*, June 14, 2012.

[77] Elaine Kurtenbach, "Companies Brace for End of Cheap Made-in-China Era," *Associated Press*, July 8, 2010; Keith Richburg, "Labor Unrest in China Reflects Changing Demographics, More Awareness of Rights," *Washington Post*, June 7, 2010.

[78] Foxconn reportedly operates more than 20 factories in China and 920,000 employees. Frederik Balfour and Tim Culpan, "Inside Foxconn," *Businessweek*, September 19, 2010.

[79] According to PRC law and policy, there is no constitutional right to strike.

[80] Li Qiaoyi, "Labor Issues Top the Agenda," *Global Times*, June 28, 2010.

[81] Fair Labor Association, "Independent Investigation of Apple Supplier, Foxconn," March 2012, http://www.fairlabor.org/sites/default/files/documents/reports/foxconn_investigation_report.pdf.

[82] Congressional-Executive Commission on China, op. cit.; "Hired Thugs Attack NGO," *Radio Free Asia*, August 31, 2012.

[83] This organization reportedly brings together associations representing both labor and industry. China Development Brief, "Local Initiatives and Incremental Measures," *Policy Brief No. 7* (July/August 2012).

[84] Chen Chenchen, "Civil Society Solid Base for Nation's Future," *Global Times*, November 4, 2012; Yu Keping, "Growing Importance of Social Innovation," *China Daily*, February 8, 2012.

[85] Guo Ting, "NGOs Join Forces to Submit Legislative Proposals," *China Development Brief No. 52* (Spring 2012).

[86] Chinese commentators often prefer to use the term "social organization" rather than "non-governmental organization" in order to avoid suggesting an adversarial relationship between society and the state. Some Western analysts use the term "civil society organization" rather than "non-governmental organization" to reflect Chinese NGOs' lack of real autonomy.

[87] Congressional-Executive Commission on China, op. cit.

[88] Ibid. Estimates of the number of Chinese social organizations vary due to differing definitions.

[89] Xu Jingxi, "Guangzhou Eases Way for Social Organizations," *China Daily*, May 7, 2012.

[90] China Development Brief, "The 18th Party Congress and China's Civil Society," *Special Policy Brief No. 10* (November 2012); Mike Frick, "Grassroots Advocacy in China: Year in Review," *Asiacatalyst.org*, December 2012.

[91] China Internet Network Information Center, *31st Statistical Report on Internet Development in China*, January 15, 2013.

[92] Committee to Protect Journalists, December 1, 2012, http://www.cpj.org/imprisoned/2012.php; Reporters without Borders, *2013 Press Freedom Index*, http://en.rsf.org/press-freedom Freedom House, *Freedom on the Net 2012*, September 24, 2012, http://www.freedomhouse.org/sites/default/files/resources FOTN%202012%20Summary%20of%20Findings.pdf.

[93] Yanqi Tong and Shaohua Lei, "Creating Public Opinion Pressure in China: Large-Scale Internet Protest," East Asian Institute (Singapore) Background Brief No. 534, June 17, 2010.

[94] Mary Kay Magistad, "How Weibo Is Changing China," *Yale Global* Online, August 9, 2012; Kathrin Hile, "China's Tweeting Cops Blog to Keep Peace," *Financial Times*, December 5, 2011; Keith B. Richburg, "In China, Microblogging Sites Become Free-Speech Platform,"

Washington Post, March 27, 2011; Ed Zhang,"Does Blogs' Blooming Mean Schools of Thought Can Contend?" *South China Morning Post*, December 4, 2011.

[95] Loretta Chao and Jason Dean, "Analysis: China Is Losing a War over Internet," *Wall Street Journal*, December 31, 2009.

[96] Rebecca MacKinnon, *Consent of the Networked*, Basic Books: New York, 2012.

[97] For further information, see CRS Report R42601, *China, Internet Freedom, and U.S. Policy*, coordinated by Thomas Lum.

[98] Amy Nip, "HK Firms Help Mainlanders Get Around the 'Great Firewall'," *South China Morning Post*, March 15, 2011.

[99] Ed Zhang,"Does Blogs' Blooming Mean Schools of Thought Can Contend?" *South China Morning Post*, December 4, 2011; Rebecca MacKinnon, "Bloggers and Censors: Chinese Media in the Internet Age," *China Studies Center*, May 18, 2007; John Pomfret, "U.S. Risks Ire with Decision to Fund Software Maker Tied to Falun Gong," *Washington Post*, May 12, 2010; MacKinnon, *Consent of the Networked*, op. cit.

[100] Joe McDonald, "China Requires Internet Users to Register Names," *Associated Press*, December 28, 2012.

[101] Catherine Shu, "Proposed Chinese Law May Force Sina Weibo to Implement Real-Name Registration," *Tech Crunch*, December 23, 2012; Josh Ong, "It's Done. China Makes It Mandatory for All Internet Users to Register with Their Real Names," *The Next Web*, December 28, 2012.

[102] Gui Tao and Huang Xin, "China Voice: Nothing to Fear from New Internet ID Policy," *English news.cn*, December 28, 2012.

[103] Calum MacLeod, "Deal Reached at Chinese Newspaper That Defied Authorities," *USA Today*, January 10, 2013; Keith Richburg, "Chinese Journalists Choose Quiet Defiance, Not Mass Strike, to Protest Censorship," *Washington Post*, January 10, 2012.

[104] Ibid; Dui Hua Foundation, *Annual Report*, May 1, 2012; "China Bans Forced Confessions in Investigations," *Xinhua*, December 26, 2012; Chris Buckley, "China Parliament Unveils Dissident Detention Powers," *Reuters*, March 8, 2012.

[105] "Prisoner Organ Donation to Be Phased Out," *South China Morning Post*, March 23, 2012; "China Accelerates Plan to Phase Out Prisoner Organ Harvesting," *Dow Jones Global Equities News*, November 2, 2012.

[106] Dui Hua Foundation, "China Under the Microscope: The Second Universal Periodic Review," February 28, 2013.

[107] Michael Bristow, "China Orders Suspension of Death Sentences," *BBC News*, May 25, 2011.

[108] Zhao Ran, "China Amends Law on State Secrets," *Global Times*, September 27, 2010; Jonathan Ansfield, "China Passes Tighter Information Law," *New York Times*, April 29, 2010.

[109] While the state owns all land in China, farmers are granted rights of use via long term (30-year) contracts with the state. Maureen Fan, "China to Allow Land Leasing, Transfer," *Washington Post*, October 20, 2008.

[110] Edward Cody, "China Announces Rules to Require Government Disclosures," *Washington Post*, April 24, 2007.

[111] Suisheng Zhao, "Political Reform in China: Toward Democracy or a Rule of Law Regime," *Asia Program Special Report No. 131*, Woodrow Wilson International Center for Scholars, June 2006; Richard Baum, "The Limits of Consultative Leninism," *Asia Program Special Report No. 131*, Woodrow Wilson International Center for Scholars, June 2006.

[112] Warren Christopher, Secretary of State under the Clinton Administration (1993-1997), stated: "Our policy will seek to facilitate a peaceful evolution of China from communism to

democracy by encouraging the forces of economic and political liberalization in that great country." Warren Christopher, Statement before the Senate Foreign Relations Committee, January 13, 1993.

[113] "Clinton Defends 'Constructive Engagement' of China," *CNN*, October 24, 1997.

[114] "Transcript of Bob Costas' Interview with President George W. Bush," *PRNewsChannel.com*, August 11, 2008; "Bush Woos China on Trade," *BBC News*, May 30, 2001.

[115] Ewen MacAskill and Tania Branigan, "Obama Presses Hu Jintao on Human Rights During White House Welcome," *Guardian.co.uk*, January 19, 2011; Helene Cooper and Mark Landler, "Obama Pushes Hu on Rights but Stresses Ties to China," *New York Times*, January 19, 2011.

[116] Pursuant to §902 of the Foreign Relations Authorization Act of 1990-1991 and §710(a) of the International Financial Institutions Act.

[117] See H.Rept. 112-331, §7044(a).

[118] See H.Rept. 112-331, §7085(c). The "Kemp-Kasten" amendment to the FY1985 Supplemental Appropriations Act (P.L. 99-88) bans U.S. assistance to organizations that support or participate in the management of coercive family planning programs. For further information, see CRS Report RL33250, *International Family Planning Programs: Issues for Congress*, by Luisa Blanchfield.

[119] Elise Labott, "Clinton Defends Stance on Human Rights," *CNN*, March 11, 2009; Charley Keyes, "U.S. is 'Pragmatic' with China, Russia," *CNN.com*, December 15, 2009; Steve Lee Myers and Mark Landler, "Behind Twists of Diplomacy in the Case of a Chinese Dissident," *New York Times*, May 9, 2012.

[120] Charles Hutzler and Jennifer Loven, "Analysis: Obama's China Trip Shows Power Shifting," *Associated Press*, November 17, 2009; Charles Hutzler and Jennifer Loven, "Obama's Visit to China Yields Few Concessions," *Associated Press*, November 18, 2009; Francois Bougon, "Obama's Visit Leaves Dissidents Disappointed," *Agence France-Presse*, November 19, 2009.

[121] Jeffrey Goldberg, "Danger: Falling Tyrants," *The Atlantic*, June 2011.

[122] Richard Wolf, "Biden Tackles Trade, Human Rights in China Visit," *USA Today*, August 21, 2011.

[123] Matthew Lee, "Hillary Clinton Presses China on Human Rights, Iran, Other Challenges," *Associated Press*, May 4, 2012.

[124] Since the U.S. government began sponsoring resolutions criticizing China's human rights record in 1991, they have been blocked by "no action" motions nearly every time. Only one, in 1995, was considered by the UNCHR, but lost by one vote. The last such U.S. resolution was introduced in 2004.

[125] See CRS Report RL33608, *The United Nations Human Rights Council: Issues for Congress*, by Luisa Blanchfield.

[126] Human Rights in China (HRIC), "China's UN Human Rights Review: New Process, Old Politics, Weak Implementation Prospects," February 9, 2009.

[127] Dui Hua Foundation, "China Under the Microscope: The Second Universal Periodic Review," op. cit.

[128] Department of State, "Conclusion of the U.S.-China Human Rights Dialogue," July 24, 2012; Department of State, "Briefing on the 17th U.S.-China Human Rights Dialogue," July 25, 2012.

[129] Li Xiaorong, "What I Told Obama About Beijing's Human Rights Problem," *The New York Review of Books*, January 18, 2011; Human Rights Watch, "China/US: Dialogue Needs to Produce Results," July 20, 2012.

[130] Department of State, "Briefing on the 17th U.S.-China Human Rights Dialogue," op. cit.

[131] Community Resources for Justice, "John Larivee Travels to China with US State Department for US- China Legal Experts Dialogue," http://www.crj.org/news/entry/john-larivee-travels-to-china-with-us-state-

[132] P.L. 106-286, Title III, Section 301.

[133] See http://www.cecc.gov.

[134] For further information, see CRS Report RS22663, *U.S. Assistance Programs in China*, by Thomas Lum.

[135] For further information, see CRS Report R42601, *China, Internet Freedom, and U.S. Policy*, coordinated by Thomas Lum.

[136] Department of State, Bureau of Democracy, Human Rights, and Labor, *Advancing Freedom and Democracy Reports,* May 2010.

[137] Interagency Working Group on U.S. Government-Sponsored International Exchanges and Training, *FY2011 U.S. Government-Sponsored International Exchanges & Training Regional Report—East Asia and Pacific*. These totals include the following programs: Post-Generated Exchange and Training; Citizen Exchange; Fulbright; Global Educational; International Visitor Leadership; Special Academic Exchange; Special Professional and Cultural Exchange; and U.S. Speaker/Specialist.

[138] NED's core institutes or grantees are the International Republican Institute (IRI); the American Center for International Labor Solidarity (ACILS); the Center for International Private Enterprise (CIPE); and the National Democratic Institute for International Affairs (NDI). For further information, see CRS Report RS22663, *U.S. Assistance Programs in China*, by Thomas Lum.

In: Human Rights in China   ISBN: 978-1-63463-180-8
Editor: Kimberly Austin   © 2014 Nova Science Publishers, Inc.

Chapter 2

CHINA 2013 HUMAN RIGHTS REPORT*

U.S. Department of State; Bureau of Democracy, Human Rights and Labor

EXECUTIVE SUMMARY

The People's Republic of China (PRC) is an authoritarian state in which the Chinese Communist Party (CCP) constitutionally is the paramount authority. CCP members hold almost all top government and security apparatus positions. Ultimate authority rests with the 25-member Political Bureau (Politburo) of the CCP and its seven-member Standing Committee. China completed its once-in-a-decade leadership transition in March, and Xi Jinping holds the three most powerful positions as CCP general secretary, state president, and chairman of the Central Military Commission. Civilian authorities generally maintained control of the military and internal security forces. Security forces committed human rights abuses.

Repression and coercion, particularly against organizations and individuals involved in civil and political rights advocacy and public interest issues, ethnic minorities, and law firms that took on sensitive cases, were routine. Increasingly officials employed harassment, intimidation, and prosecution of family members and associates to retaliate against rights

---

* This is an edited, reformatted and augmented version of a report released by the U.S. Department of State; Bureau of Democracy, Human Rights and Labor, updated March 21, 2014.

advocates and defenders. Individuals and groups seen as politically sensitive by authorities continued to face tight restrictions on their freedom to assemble, practice religion, and travel. Authorities resorted to extralegal measures such as enforced disappearance and strict house arrest, including house arrest of family members, to prevent public expression of independent opinions. Authorities implemented new measures to control and censor the internet and particularly targeted bloggers with large numbers of followers, leading some to close their online accounts. Public-interest law firms continued to face harassment, disbarment of legal staff, and closure. There was severe official repression of the freedoms of speech, religion, association, and assembly of ethnic Uighurs in the Xinjiang Uighur Autonomous Region (XUAR) and of ethnic Tibetans in the Tibet Autonomous Region (TAR) and other Tibetan areas. These minorities also faced harsh restrictions on movement. Abuses peaked around high-profile events, such as the visit of foreign officials, national meetings, and commemorations.

As in previous years, citizens did not have the right to change their government, and citizens had limited forms of redress against official abuse. Other human rights problems during the year included extrajudicial killings, including executions without due process; enforced disappearance and incommunicado detention, including prolonged illegal detentions at unofficial holding facilities known as "black jails"; torture and coerced confessions of prisoners; detention and harassment of lawyers, journalists, writers, bloggers, dissidents, petitioners, and others who sought to exercise peacefully their rights under the law; a lack of due process in judicial proceedings; political control of courts and judges; closed trials; the use of administrative detention; restrictions on freedom to assemble, practice religion, and travel; failure to protect refugees and asylum seekers; pressure on other countries to return PRC citizens forcibly; widespread corruption; intense scrutiny of and restrictions on nongovernmental organizations (NGOs); discrimination against women, minorities, and persons with disabilities; a coercive birth-limitation policy that in some cases resulted in forced abortion (sometimes at advanced stages of pregnancy) or forced sterilization; trafficking in persons; prohibitions on independent unions; lack of protection for workers' right to strike; forced and child labor; and poor enforcement of wage, overtime, and occupational safety and health laws.

Although authorities prosecuted a number of abuses of power, particularly with regard to corruption, in many cases the internal disciplinary procedures of the CCP were opaque and only selectively applied to senior officials. Citizens who promoted efforts to combat corruption were themselves detained and arrested. For example, throughout the year, NGO sources reported that authorities arrested at least 29 persons associated with the New Citizens Movement on charges stemming from activities to promote good governance.

SECTION 1. RESPECT FOR THE INTEGRITY OF THE PERSON, INCLUDING FREEDOM FROM

a. Arbitrary or Unlawful Deprivation of Life

During the year security forces reportedly committed arbitrary or unlawful killings. In many instances few or no details were available.

It was not clear to what extent impunity was a problem. Following cases of killings by police, there often was an announcement that an investigation was to be conducted, but it was not clear whether there were any findings of police malfeasance or any cases in which police were disciplined.

For example, on October 24, plainclothes police arrested Shanghai petitioner Shen Yong for trespassing and, according to media reports, beat him. Hours later police returned Shen to his family, and he died shortly thereafter. Shen's family maintained he died as a result of the police beating. Police asserted he suddenly fell ill in their custody. Local media reported that the death was under investigation but by year's end provided no further information. Authorities detained more than 100 petitioners at a protest following Shen's death.

A number of violent incidents in the XUAR resulted in multiple deaths. Official accounts of these events generally blamed "terrorists," "separatists," and "religious extremists" for what were portrayed as violent terrorist attacks on community members and security personnel. Human rights organizations, on the other hand, asserted that security forces often shot at groups of Uighurs in their homes or during worship. The government's control of information coming out of the XUAR, together with its increasingly tight security posture there, made it difficult to verify the conflicting reports.

For example on April 24, at least 21 persons were killed in a clash in Barchuk County, XUAR: nine bystanders, six police, and six Uighurs (described in the official press as "thugs"). According to the official account, gunfights broke out when police entered persons' homes to search for "illegal knives."

In April, Yu Qiyi, a chief engineer at a state-owned enterprise in Wenzhou, died after being interrogated for corruption. Authorities arrested six CCP investigators and convicted them of intentional assault (see section 1.d.).

Defendants in criminal proceedings were executed following convictions that lacked due process and adequate channels for appeal.

b. Disappearance

In September authorities detained Cao Shunli at Beijing Airport as she was attempting to travel to Geneva to attend a training session in advance of China's Universal Periodic Review at the UN Human Rights Council. Five weeks after her disappearance, authorities at the Chaoyang District Detention Center confirmed that Cao had been criminally detained on charges of unlawful assembly. According to various media reports, her family did not received a detention notice in accordance with the Criminal Procedure Law.

At year's end the government had not provided a comprehensive, credible accounting of all those killed, missing, or detained in connection with the violent suppression of the 1989 Tiananmen demonstrations. It is estimated that fewer than a dozen remained in prison, although some accounts suggest the number may be higher. Many activists who were involved in the demonstrations continued to suffer from official harassment.

c. Torture and Other Cruel, Inhuman, or Degrading Treatment or Punishment

The law prohibits the physical abuse of detainees and forbids prison guards from extracting confessions by torture, insulting prisoners' dignity, and beating or encouraging others to beat prisoners. Amendments to the criminal procedure law that exclude evidence, including confessions, obtained through illegal means, including under torture in certain categories of criminal cases, took effect on January 1.

Numerous former prisoners and detainees reported that they were beaten, subjected to electric shock, forced to sit on stools for hours on end, deprived of sleep, and otherwise subjected to physical and psychological abuse. Although ordinary prisoners were subjects of abuse, prison authorities singled out political and religious dissidents for particularly harsh treatment. In some instances close relatives of dissidents also were singled out for abuse.

Human Rights Watch reported that police beat and tortured suspected prostitutes.

According to news reports Xiao Yong, a Guangzhou-based activist detained by police in April 2012 and remanded to two years of re-education through labor (RTL) in Shaoyang, Hunan Province, was released in February and allowed to return to his home. Authorities charged him with illegal assembly for staging a demonstration calling on officials to disclose publicly their financial assets. During his initial detention authorities reportedly prevented Xiao from sleeping for up to five days, causing multiple medical complications.

On May 18, police arrested a group of Fujian activists. Police held petitioner Lin Yingqiang for 33 hours, deprived him of food, and chained him to a "tiger seat," a device meant to prevent the prisoner from sleeping during his detention.

In May authorities in Sichuan Province detained and beat lawyers Tang Jitian and Jiang Tianyong as they attempted to visit a black jail in Ziyang that reportedly holds followers of the banned Falun Gong movement.

On June 8, the Dongcheng District People's Court tried Peng Lanlan in closed proceedings. The court's decision was not available at year's end. Beijing police arrested Peng in August 2012, charged him with obstructing official business, and tortured him by binding him to a tiger seat.

There were widespread reports of activists and petitioners being committed to mental-health facilities and involuntarily subjected to psychiatric treatment for political reasons. According to *Legal Daily* (a state-owned newspaper covering legal affairs), the Ministry of Public Security directly administered 24 high-security psychiatric hospitals for the criminally insane (also known as ankang facilities). From 1998 to May 2010, more than 40,000 persons were committed to ankang hospitals. In 2010 an official of the Ministry of Public Security stated that detention in ankang facilities was not appropriate for patients who did not demonstrate criminal behavior. Nonetheless, political activists, underground religious adherents, persons who repeatedly petitioned the government, members of the banned Chinese Democracy Party (CDP), and Falun Gong practitioners were among those housed in these institutions.

In October 2012 the government passed legislation banning involuntary mental health examinations and inpatient treatment except in cases in which patients expressed an intent to harm themselves or others. Critics maintained, however, that the law still does not provide meaningful legal protections for persons sent to psychiatric facilities. The March 2012 amendments to the criminal procedure law require a procuratorate (the agency responsible for both prosecution and investigation) review and a court decision for the psychiatric commitment of persons who have committed serious offenses but are exempt from criminal responsibility under the law. The amendments went into effect in April and include a provision for appealing compulsory medical treatment decisions.

On April 7, a new mainland China magazine *Lens* carried an article reporting abuses including torture with electric batons, forced feeding, and prolonged solitary confinement at the Masanjia Detention Center in Liaoning Province.

Advocacy groups continued to report organ harvesting from prisoners. Former vice health minister Huang Jiefu, who in March 2012 reportedly pledged to abolish taking organs for transplant from executed prisoners within three to five years, stated that organs from executed prisoners accounted for 64 percent of transplants in 2012 and for 54 percent in mid-2013.

Prison and Detention Center Conditions

Conditions in penal institutions for both political prisoners and criminal offenders were generally harsh and often degrading.

Forced labor remained a serious problem in penal institutions (see section 7.b.) as well as in RTL facilities. On December 28, the National People's Congress (NPC) Standing Committee passed legislation that formally abolished the RTL system. State media announced that all inmates would be released beginning December 30 and clarified that all pre-abolition penalties would be considered legitimate. On December 17, Amnesty International reported that authorities relabeled many RTL camps as "drug rehabilitation centers" and "legal education centers."

Physical Conditions: Prisoners and detainees were regularly held in overcrowded conditions with poor sanitation. Food often was inadequate and of poor quality, and many detainees relied on supplemental food, medicines, and warm clothing provided by relatives. Prisoners often reported sleeping on the floor because there were no beds or bedding. Adequate, timely medical care for prisoners remained a serious problem, despite official assurances that prisoners have the right to prompt medical treatment.

Information on the prison population was not made public. In an April 2012 report to the NPC Standing Committee, the minister of justice stated that the country had 681 prisons with 1.64 million inmates. The International Center for Prison Studies (ICPS) reported that in 2009, in addition to sentenced prisoners, 650,000 persons were held in detention centers, and it estimated there were between 100,000 and 260,000 pretrial detainees. The ICPS reported that in mid-2010 female prisoners made up approximately 5.1 percent of the prison population, and in 2005 juveniles made up 1.4 percent. The law requires juveniles be held separately from adults, unless facilities are insufficient, but children were sometimes held with adult prisoners and required to work. Political prisoners were held with the general prison population and reported being beaten by other prisoners at the instigation of guards. Some dissidents were not allowed to receive supplemental food, medicine, and warm clothing from relatives.

The law mandates that a prison shall be ventilated, allow for natural light, and be clean and warm. The law further provides that a prison "shall set up medical, living, and sanitary facilities and institute regulations on the life and sanitation of prisoners." It also states that the medical and health care of prisoners shall be put into the public health and epidemic prevention program of the area in which the prison is located. In many cases provisions for sanitation, ventilation, heating, lighting, basic and emergency medical care, and access to potable water were inadequate.

Conditions in administrative detention facilities, such as RTL camps, were similar to those in prisons. Beating deaths occurred in administrative detention and RTL facilities. Detainees reported beatings, sexual assaults, lack of proper food, and limited or no access to medical care.

Administration: It was unclear whether recordkeeping on prisoners was adequate. Authorities employed alternatives to incarceration for both violent and nonviolent offenders. According to Vice Minister of Justice Zhao Dacheng, more than one million convicts served their sentences in community corrections programs since 2003. There were no prison ombudsmen per se, but prisoners and detainees are legally entitled to submit complaints to judicial authorities without censorship and request investigation of credible allegations of inhuman conditions. The law states that letters from a prisoner to higher authorities of the prison or to the judicial organs shall be free from examination, but it was unclear to what extent the law was implemented. While authorities occasionally investigated credible allegations of inhuman conditions, the results were not documented in a publicly accessible manner. Many prisoners and detainees did not have reasonable access to visitors and could not engage in religious practices. Under Article 52 of the prison law, "considerations shall be given to the special habits and customs of prisoners of minority ethnic groups." Article 23 of the Detention Center Regulation has similar requirements. Little information was available about the implementation of these regulations.

The law requires the government to investigate and monitor prison and detention center conditions, and an official from the Prosecutor's Office is responsible for investigating and monitoring prison and detention center conditions.

Independent Monitoring: Information about prisons, including associated labor camps and factories, was considered a state secret, and the government did not permit independent monitoring of prisons or RTL camps. Prisoners remained inaccessible to local and international human rights organizations and media groups. Authorities did not allow the International Committee of the Red Cross to have access to prisoners or perform prison visits in the country.

d. Arbitrary Arrest or Detention

Arbitrary arrest and detention remained serious problems. The law grants police broad administrative detention powers and the ability to detain individuals for extended periods without formal arrest or criminal charges. Throughout the year human rights activists, journalists, unregistered religious leaders, and former political prisoners and their family members continued to be among those targeted for arbitrary detention or arrest.

In January the official media reported that authorities in Heilongjiang Province confined petitioner Chen Qingxia to a deserted mortuary for three years. Chen previously served 18-months' in RTL, was allegedly paralyzed by repeated beatings, and separated from her then 12-year-old son by local authorities. After the media report the local government reportedly found a house for Chen and pledged to help her look for her son.

From June 3 to 25, in Shenyang, Liaoning Province, plainclothes police reportedly detained prodemocracy activist Jiang Lijun on suspicion of inciting subversion of state authority and disturbing the social order. Jiang previously served a four-year sentence for "inciting subversion of the state power."

In July, Guangdong activist Wu Bin, also known as Xiucai Jianghu, was detained for allegedly "sabotaging electric power equipment." Wu previously filed a lawsuit against Shenzhen's Futian District Public Security Bureau (PSB) for illegally detaining him. He was released on bail in early August, rearrested in Zhejiang Province on September 12, and given 10 days' administrative detention for "spreading rumors."

Many activists were subjected to extralegal house arrest, denied travel rights, or administratively detained. Shanghai dissidents Feng Zhenghu and Zheng Enchong were under unofficial house arrest at their apartments in Shanghai. Both were allowed to move around Shanghai on occasion but were kept under constant surveillance. Outsiders were often prevented from visiting them, and they were not allowed to leave Shanghai. Zheng Enchong was denied permission to travel to Hong Kong to accept a fellowship teaching law. Authorities also reportedly kept other dissidents under unofficial house arrest. Officials sentenced Shanghai activists Wang Kouma and Wei Qin to 30 months and 27 months in prison, respectively, for "creating a disturbance" related to their lawful petitioning. Mao Hengfeng was released from RTL on February 8 and was serving the remainder of her 18-month sentence under house arrest.

Role of the Police and Security Apparatus

The main domestic security agencies include the Ministry of State Security, the Ministry of Public Security, and the People's Armed Police. The People's Liberation Army is primarily responsible for external security but also has some domestic security responsibilities. Local jurisdictions also frequently used civilian municipal security forces, known as "urban management" officials (chengguan), to enforce administrative measures. The Ministry of Public Security coordinates the country's civilian police force, which is organized into specialized police agencies and local, county, and provincial jurisdictions. Procuratorate oversight of the police was limited. Corruption at the local level was widespread. Police and urban management officials engaged in extrajudicial detention, extortion, and assault. In 2009 the Supreme People's Procuratorate acknowledged continuing widespread abuse in law enforcement. In 2009 domestic news media reported the convictions of public security officials who had beaten to death prisoners or suspects in their custody.

In May 2012 the Ministry of Supervision, Ministry of Human Resources and Social Security, and Ministry of Justice jointly issued regulations stating that police in prisons and RTL facilities face dismissal if they are found to have beaten, applied corporal punishment, abused inmates, or instigated such acts.

There were several media reports on deaths under the shuanggui system – the CCP internal disciplinary system used to investigate party members suspected of corruption. In April, Yu Qiyi, a chief engineer at a state-owned enterprise in Wenzhou, died after being interrogated for corruption.

Authorities charged six investigators from the Communist Party's Disciplinary Committee in Wenzhou. The BBC reported they were sentenced to between four and 14 years in prison. They reportedly appealed their sentence.

Oversight of civilian municipal security forces was highly localized and ad hoc. By law the officials can be criminally prosecuted for abuses of power, but such cases were rarely pursued. There were multiple reports of conflicts erupting between these officials and street vendors in Liaoning, Jilin, and Heilongjiang provinces. For example, on June 19, civilian municipal security forces reportedly beat a family of fried-chicken vendors in the Beihang night market in Shenyang, Liaoning Province, who refused to turn over their equipment. In protest more than one thousand Shenyang residents gathered at the scene and blocked traffic, and some reportedly retaliated by beating the officials. In some cases mediation resulted in compensation being paid to victims of these officials.

Arrest Procedures and Treatment of Detainees

Police detention beyond 37 days requires prosecutorial approval of a formal arrest. After arrest police are authorized to detain a suspect for up to an additional seven months while the case is investigated.

After the completion of a police investigation, an additional 45 days of detention are allowed for the procuratorate to determine whether to file criminal charges. If charges are filed authorities can detain a suspect for an additional 45 days before beginning judicial proceedings. Police sometimes detained persons beyond the period allowed by law, and pretrial detention periods of a year or longer were common.

The law stipulates that detainees be allowed to meet with defense counsel before criminal charges are filed. Some criminal defense attorneys noted that under the newly revised criminal procedure law their ability to meet with clients improved significantly. In some cases defense attorneys were able to arrange visits at any time and to have private meetings with their clients in detention centers. This generally did not apply to cases considered politically sensitive.

The criminal procedure law requires a court to provide a lawyer to a defendant who has not already retained one; who is blind, deaf, mute, or a minor; or who may be sentenced to death. Revisions that took effect on January 1 added defendants facing a life sentence or who are mentally ill. This law applies whether or not the defendant is indigent. Courts may also provide lawyers to other criminal defendants who cannot afford them, although courts often did not appoint counsel in such circumstances.

Criminal defendants are entitled to apply for bail (also translated as "a guarantor pending trial") while awaiting trial, but the system does not appear to operate effectively and few suspects were released on bail.

The law requires notification of family members within 24 hours of detention, but individuals were often held without notification for significantly longer periods, especially in politically sensitive cases. Under a sweeping exception officials are not required to provide notification if doing so would "hinder the investigation" of a case. The revised criminal procedure law limits this exception to cases involving state security or terrorism.

The law allows for residential surveillance rather than detention in a formal facility under certain circumstances. Under the revised criminal procedure law, with the approval of the next higher-level authorities, officials can enforce "residential surveillance" on a suspect at a designated place of residence (i.e., a place other than the suspect's home) for up to six months, when they suspect crimes of endangering state security, terrorism, or serious bribery and believe that surveillance at the suspect's residence would impede the investigation. Authorities must notify relatives of individuals placed under formal arrest or residential surveillance in a designated abode within 24 hours, unless notification is impossible. They are not required to specify the grounds for or location of the detention. Authorities can also prevent defense lawyers from meeting with suspects in these categories of cases.

The law provides for the right to petition the government for resolution of grievances, but citizens who traveled to Beijing to petition the central government were frequently subjected to arbitrary detention, often by police dispatched from the petitioner's hometown. Some provincial governments operated facilities in Beijing or in other localities where petitioners from their districts were held in extrajudicial detention. Some local governments took steps to restrict petitioning. According to a 2010 Shanxi provincial government report, the Shanxi Province People's Congress adopted regulations that listed eight types of "prohibited" petitioning, including: "illegally gathering, encircling, or rushing into government offices or important public spaces, stopping cars or hindering public transportation, linking up with others to petition," and similar acts. The Shanxi regulations also stated that petitioners suspected of "misrepresenting facts to frame others" could be subject to criminal charges.

Online reports claimed local officials in Zengcheng City, Guangdong Province, sealed off two villages in March during the People's Congress and the Chinese People's Political Consultative Conference (CPPCC) sessions to prevent residents from petitioning.

On April 17, Shenzhen-based lawyer Jiang Yuanmin was arrested and charged with "gathering a crowd to disrupt social order" in connection with his work on behalf of Hainan farmers' land rights, according to online reports. Family members claimed he was denied medical treatment.

Fujian petitioner Luo Xianying was reportedly arrested in Beijing in fall 2012 and forcibly returned to Sanming in November 2012. At year's end she was detained in a government building, and her family claimed she had not received adequate treatment for her medical problems.

Before the December 28 NPC Standing Committee decision to abolish RTL, nonjudicial panels, known as "labor re-education panels," could remand persons to RTL camps for up to three years without trial. Labor re-education panels were authorized to extend these administrative sentences for up to one year. Detainees were technically allowed to challenge administrative RTL sentences and appeal for sentence reduction or suspension, but appeals were rarely successful.

Other forms of administrative detention include "custody and education" (for women engaged in prostitution and those soliciting prostitution) and "custody and training" (for minor criminal offenders). The law establishes a system of "compulsory isolation for drug rehabilitation." The minimum stay in such centers is two years, and the law states that treatment can include labor. Public security organs authorize detention in these centers, and it often was meted out as an administrative rather than criminal measure. Authorities used administrative detention to intimidate political activists and prevent public demonstrations.

Arbitrary Arrest: In February police began detaining and arresting dozens of activists, lawyers, and other citizens in an apparently coordinated crackdown on a loose grouping of activists known as the New Citizens Movement. The Beijing Municipality Traffic Security Division detained Beijing University of Post and Telecommunications lecturer and legal scholar Xu Zhiyong on July 16 on suspicion of "gathering a crowd to disturb public order." He was formally arrested on August 22 and formally charged in December. On September 13, authorities detained venture capitalist and popular microblogger Wang Gongquan on charges of "gathering a crowd to disturb public order," after he used his microblog to decry Xu's arrest.

Other New Citizens Movement associates arrested for peaceful advocacy of good governance included Liu Ping, Wei Zhongping, Li Sihua, Yuan Dong, Ma Xinli, Zhang Baocheng, Hou Xin, Li Wei, Wang Yonghong, Ding Jiaxi,

Sun Hanhui, Zhao Changqing, Qi Yueying, Zhang Xiangzhong, Li Gang, Li Huanjun, and Song Guangqiang.

Authorities arrested persons on allegations of revealing state secrets, subversion, and other crimes as a means to suppress political dissent and public advocacy. These charges – including what constitutes a state secret – remained ill defined. Authorities also detained citizens and foreigners under broad and ambiguous state secrets laws for, among other actions, disclosing information on criminal trials, meetings, commercial activity, and government activity. Authorities sometimes retroactively labeled a particular action as a violation of the state secret laws. According to a Radio Free Asia (RFA) report, local officials in Dujiangyan, Sichuan Province, detained Zhou Xingrong, whose child died in the 2008 Sichuan earthquake, for nine hours in April 2012 for allegedly revealing "state secrets" by microblogging about efforts by bereaved parents to obtain compensation for their children's earthquake-related deaths. According to a western media report, authorities continued to harass her during the year.

Authorities placed numerous dissidents, activists, and petitioners under house arrest during the October National Day holiday period and at other sensitive times, such as during the visits of senior foreign government officials or in the period preceding the annual plenary sessions of the NPC and the CPPCC, the anniversary of the Tiananmen massacre, and sensitive anniversaries in Tibetan areas and the XUAR.

Conditions faced by those under house arrest varied but sometimes included complete isolation in their homes under police guard. In some instances security officials were stationed inside the homes of subjects under house arrest. Others under house arrest occasionally were permitted to leave their homes to work or run errands but were required to ride in police vehicles. In some cases police or plainclothes security officers escorted the children of politically sensitive individuals to and from school. When permitted to leave their homes, subjects of house arrest were usually under police surveillance. Authorities in the XUAR used house arrest and other forms of arbitrary detention against those accused of supporting the "three evils" of religious extremism, "splittism," and terrorism.

After serving one year at an RTL camp for staging protests calling for political reforms and attempting to visit prominent activist Ai Weiwei, Fujian petitioner Wang Weizhu was released in July. She went to a foreign embassy compound in Beijing after her release to distribute leaflets about her grievances, after which Beijing Police reportedly detained her for five days.

According to the RFA, in June authorities detained members of the Guizhou Human Rights Symposium, including Wu Yuqin, Li Renke, and Mo Jiangang, and forced them to leave the provincial capital for the duration of the two-day EU-China meeting on human rights there.

Pretrial Detention: Pretrial detention can last as long as one year. Defendants in "sensitive cases" reported being subjected to prolonged pretrial detention.

e. Denial of Fair Public Trial

The law states that the courts shall exercise judicial power independently, without interference from administrative organs, social organizations, and individuals. The judiciary did not exercise judicial power independently. Legal scholars interpreted former president Hu Jintao's doctrine of the "Three Supremes" as stating that the interests of the CCP are above the law. Judges regularly received political guidance on pending cases, including instructions on how to rule, from both the government and the CCP, particularly in politically sensitive cases. The CCP Law and Politics Committee has the authority to review and influence court operations at all levels of the judiciary.

During the year media sources indicated public security authorities used televised confessions of foreign and domestic bloggers, journalists, and business executives in an attempt to establish guilt before their criminal trial proceedings began.

A CCP-controlled committee decides most major cases, and the duty of trial and appellate court judges is to craft a legal justification for the committee's decision.

"Judicial independence" was reportedly one of the off-limit subjects that the CCP ordered university professors not to discuss (see section 2.a., Academic Freedom).

Corruption also influenced court decisions. Safeguards against judicial corruption were vague and poorly enforced. Local governments appoint and pay local court judges and, as a result, often exerted influence over the rulings of judges in their districts.

Courts are not authorized to rule on the constitutionality of legislation. The law permits organizations or individuals to question the constitutionality of laws and regulations, but a constitutional challenge can be directed only to the promulgating legislative body. Lawyers have little or no opportunity to rely on constitutional claims in litigation.

Trial Procedures

The criminal justice system was biased toward a presumption of guilt, especially in high-profile or politically sensitive cases. According to the Supreme People's Court, in 2011 the combined conviction rate for first- and second-instance criminal trials was 99.9 percent. Of 1,051,638 criminal defendants tried in 2011, only 891 were acquitted.

In many politically sensitive trials courts handed down guilty verdicts immediately following proceedings with no deliberation. Courts often punished defendants who refused to acknowledge guilt with harsher sentences than those who confessed. The appeals process rarely reversed convictions. Appeals processes failed to provide sufficient avenues for review, and remedies for violations of defendants' rights were inadequate.

Regulations of the Supreme People's Court require all trials to be open to the public, with the exceptions of cases involving state secrets, privacy issues, and minors. Authorities used the state-secrets provision to keep politically sensitive proceedings closed to the public, sometimes even to family members, and to withhold access to defense counsel. Court regulations state that foreigners with valid identification should be allowed to observe trials under the same criteria as citizens, but foreigners were permitted to attend court proceedings only by invitation. As in past years, foreign diplomats and journalists unsuccessfully sought permission to attend a number of trials. In some instances the trials were reclassified as "state secrets" cases or otherwise closed to the public. During the year foreign diplomats attempted to attend nearly one dozen public trials throughout the country. In each instance court officials claimed that there were no available seats in the courtroom and that foreigners needed prior permission to attend trials.

Some trials were broadcast, and court proceedings were a regular television feature. A few courts published their verdicts on the internet.

The revised criminal procedure law makes clear that a criminal suspect may retain a lawyer immediately after an initial police interrogation or after his or her freedom has been officially limited. Investigators are required to inform suspects of their right to retain counsel. Police must also arrange meetings between a defense lawyer and his or her client within 48 hours of a request from defense counsel.

Individuals facing administrative detention do not have the right to seek legal counsel. Criminal defendants were eligible for legal assistance, although more than 50 percent of criminal defendants went to trial without a lawyer. According to the Ministry of Justice, in 2012 there were more than one million legal aid cases. The revised criminal procedure law expanded requirements for legal aid to include cases that could result in life imprisonment and cases involving individuals suffering from mental illness.

Human rights lawyers reported that authorities did not permit them to defend certain clients or threatened them with punishment if they chose to do so. The government suspended or revoked the licenses of lawyers or their firms to stop them from taking sensitive cases, such as defending prodemocracy dissidents, house-church activists, Falun Gong practitioners, or government critics.

The CCP continued to require law firms with three or more CCP members to form a CCP unit within the firm. Firms with one or two CCP members may establish joint CCP units with other firms. In smaller counties and cities with few lawyers, CCP members may join local Justice Bureau CCP units. This rule also applies to private companies and other organizations.

Some lawyers declined to represent defendants in politically sensitive cases, and such defendants frequently found it difficult to find an attorney.

Authorities detained Guangzhou-based activist Yang Maodong (also known under the pen name Guo Feixiong) on August 8 on suspicion of "gathering a crowd to disrupt order of a public place." According to several Western media sources, officials repeatedly denied him access to lawyers. International media speculated he was detained in connection with his participation in protests surrounding the incident in January involving censorship of the Guangzhou newspaper *Southern Weekend* and his association with the New Citizens Movement (see section 2, Freedom of Speech and Press).

When defendants were able to retain counsel in politically sensitive cases, government officials sometimes prevented attorneys from organizing an effective defense. Tactics employed by court and government officials included unlawful detentions, disbarment, harassment and physical intimidation, and denial of access to evidence and to clients.

In April a court in Jiangsu Province placed Beijing rights lawyer Wang Quanzhang under a 10-day judicial detention for "serious violations of court procedure." The violations consisted of using his mobile telephone to copy a set of original documents he was submitting to the court during the trial of a Falun Gong practitioner.

Online reports indicated that on June 25 riot police in Wenchang, Hainan Province, intercepted a group of Guangzhou-based lawyers who had come to represent detained dissident Zheng Qiuwu and his wife. The riot police scuffled with the lawyers and forced them to return to the provincial capital of Haikou.

The annual licensing review process administered by the Beijing Lawyers Association was used to withhold or delay the renewal of professional lawyers' licenses, which restricted the ability of a number of human rights and public interest lawyers to practice law.

Government officials continued to harass lawyers for their involvement in high-profile, rights-related cases.

Defense attorneys may be held legally responsible if their client commits perjury, and prosecutors and judges have wide discretion to decide what constitutes perjury. In some sensitive cases lawyers had no pretrial access to their clients, and defendants and lawyers were not allowed to communicate with one another during trials. Criminal defendants were frequently not assigned an attorney until a case was brought to court. According to a Ministry of Justice official, in 2011 lawyers represented fewer than half of criminal defendants, and in some provincial-level administrative regions, only an estimated 12 percent of criminal suspects had lawyers.

Mechanisms allowing defendants to confront their accusers were inadequate. Only a small percentage of trials involved witnesses, and fewer than 10 percent of subpoenaed witnesses appeared in court. A provision of the revised criminal procedure law compels witnesses to appear in court and includes protections for witnesses and financial allowances for performing the duties of a witness. In most criminal trials, prosecutors read witness statements, which neither the defendants nor their lawyers had an opportunity to rebut. Although the law states that pretrial witness statements cannot serve as the sole basis for conviction, prosecutors relied heavily on such statements. Defense attorneys had no authority to compel witnesses to testify or to mandate discovery, although they could apply for access to government-held evidence relevant to their case. Defense attorneys received minimal pretrial access to information.

The criminal code contains 55 capital offenses, including nonviolent financial crimes such as embezzlement and corruption. There was no publicly available government information on how many defendants were either sentenced to death or executed during the year. Official figures on execution are classified as a state secret. An international human rights NGO estimated that 4,000 persons were executed annually in recent years, a marked decrease in the years following the 2007 Supreme People's Court retrieval of its authority to conduct final reviews of death sentences. Lethal injection and shooting were employed as execution methods.

Chen Youxi, the attorney for street vendor Xia Junfeng, who was convicted of killing two urban management officials in Shenyang, Liaoning

Province, and executed on September 25, argued that the Supreme People's Court failed to consider evidence supporting Xia's claims of self-defense during its review of his sentence. According to a report, the presiding judge refused to admit the testimony of several eyewitnesses and relied on the statements of other urban management officials.

Political Prisoners and Detainees

Government officials continued to deny holding any political prisoners, asserting that authorities detained persons not for their political or religious views but because they violated the law. Authorities, however, continued to imprison citizens for reasons related to politics and religion. Tens of thousands of political prisoners remained incarcerated, some in prisons and others in RTL camps or administrative detention. The government did not grant international humanitarian organizations access to political prisoners.

Foreign NGOs estimated that several hundred persons remained in prison for "counterrevolutionary crimes," which were removed from the criminal code in 1997. Thousands of others were serving sentences under state security statutes. The government apparently neither reviewed all cases of those charged before 1997 with counterrevolutionary crimes nor released persons jailed for nonviolent offenses under repealed provisions of the criminal law. The government maintained that prisoners serving sentences for counterrevolutionary crimes and endangering state security were eligible to apply for sentence reduction and parole. Political prisoners, however, were granted early release at lower rates than other prisoners. Observers believed that persons remained in prison for crimes in connection with their involvement in the 1989 Tiananmen prodemocracy movement, although the number was unknown because related official statistics were never made public.

Rights lawyer Gao Zhisheng remained in prison in Xinjiang for allegedly violating the terms of a suspended prison sentence. Authorities sharply limited access to him and at times concealed his whereabouts. Democracy activist Hada remained in unofficial detention in Inner Mongolia three years after reportedly completing a15-year sentence in 2010. Hada's wife and sons also faced periods of extralegal house arrest.

Many political prisoners remained in prison or under other forms of detention at year's end, including rights activists Wang Bingzhang and Liu Xianbin; Ablikim Abdureyim, son of Uighur activist Rebiya Kadeer; Zhou Yongjun; labor activist Kong Youping; Roman Catholic bishop Su Zhimin;

and Tibetan Buddhist reincarnate lama Tenzin Delek Rinpoche, who was reportedly in poor health.

Nobel Peace Prize laureate Liu Xiaobo, coauthor of the Charter '08 manifesto that called for increased political freedoms and human rights, remained in Jinzhou Prison in Liaoning Province. Beijing-based human rights attorney Mo Shaoping, whose firm represented Liu, reported that Liu's wife Liu Xia was allowed to travel from Beijing to Jinzhou to see him monthly. She remained under 24-hour surveillance, and police escorted her whenever she was allowed to leave her home. Media reports in December indicated that Liu Xia might be suffering from depression due to her long-term isolation and deprivation of access to books and the internet.

On August 16, a Beijing court sentenced Liu Hui, Liu Xiaobo's brother-in-law, to 11 years' imprisonment on spurious charges of contract fraud by. Liu Xia was allowed to attend the trial on April 23 and told onlookers outside the court that she was not free.

At year's end reliable information was not available as to whether the following individuals remained in detention: Abdulla Jamal, Uighur activist Dilkex Tilivaldi, Feng Xinchun, Gonpo Lhundrub, Gonpo Thar, Jalo, Tselo, and Wang Diangang.

Criminal punishments continued to include "deprivation of political rights" for a fixed period after release from prison, during which time the individual was denied rights of free speech, association, and publication. Former prisoners reported that their ability to find employment, travel, obtain residence permits, rent residences, and access social services was severely restricted. Former political prisoners and their families frequently were subjected to police surveillance, telephone wiretaps, searches, and other forms of harassment or threats.

Civil Judicial Procedures and Remedies

Courts deciding civil matters faced the same limitations on judicial independence as criminal courts. The State Compensation Law provides administrative and judicial remedies for plaintiffs whose rights or interests government agencies or officials have infringed. The law also allows compensation for wrongful detention, mental trauma, or physical injuries inflicted by detention center or prison officials. Citizens seldom applied for state compensation because of the high cost of bringing lawsuits, low credibility of courts, and citizens' lack of awareness of the State Compensation Law. Victims' claims were difficult to assess because of vague definitions in the law and difficulties in obtaining evidence of injury or damage. Judges were reluctant to accept state compensation cases, and government agencies seldom implemented court judgments in favor of plaintiffs.

f. Arbitrary Interference with Privacy, Family, Home, or Correspondence

While the law states that the "freedom and privacy of correspondence of citizens are protected by law," authorities often did not respect the privacy of citizens. Although the law requires warrants before law enforcement officials can search premises, officials frequently ignored this requirement. The Public Security Bureau and prosecutors are authorized to issue search warrants on their own authority without judicial review. Cases of forced entry by police officers continued to be reported.

Authorities monitored telephone conversations, fax transmissions, e-mail, text messaging, and internet communications. They also opened and censored domestic and international mail. Security services routinely monitored and entered residences and offices to gain access to computers, telephones, and fax machines.

According to foreign media reports, the Ministry of Public Security used tens of millions of surveillance cameras in the country. Authorities justified the security cameras as a way to improve public safety, crime fighting, traffic management, and "social stability." Human rights groups stated authorities increasingly relied on the cameras to monitor and intimidate political dissidents, Tibetans, and Uighurs.

The monitoring and disruption of telephone and internet communications were particularly widespread in the XUAR and Tibetan areas. Authorities frequently warned dissidents and activists, underground religious figures, and former political prisoners throughout the country not to meet with foreign journalists or diplomats, especially before sensitive anniversaries, at the time of important government or CCP meetings, and during the visits of high-level foreign officials. Security personnel harassed and detained the family members of political prisoners, including following them to meetings with foreign reporters and diplomats and urging them to remain silent about the cases of their relatives.

Family members of activists, dissidents, Falun Gong practitioners, journalists, unregistered religious figures, and former political prisoners were targeted for arbitrary arrest, detention, and harassment (see section 1.d.).

In April four unidentified men forcibly removed 10-year-old Zhang Anni, the daughter of prodemocracy activist, Zhang Lin, from school and detained her at the Hefei city police station for several hours. Under government pressure, Hupo Elementary School refused to enroll Zhang Anni for seven weeks.

Chen Kegui, nephew of activist Chen Guangcheng, remained in prison at year's end. In April media reported that Kegui was suffering from an unknown health condition in prison following allegations of torture by prison authorities. Authorities denied his family's request for medical parole.

On August 16, Guangzhou police prohibited activist Tang Jingling and his wife Wang Yanfang from attending the funeral of well known house church pastor Samuel Lamb. Security officials reportedly put many pastors under house arrest to prevent them from attending the funeral. Guangzhou security personnel had previously detained Wang Yanfang for 10 days in December 2011 and January 2012 in connection with protests in the Guangdong village of Wukan.

On May 31, police in Wenchang, Hainan, arrested dissident Zheng Qiuwu's wife. On June 4, Zhejiang authorities detained Zheng himself and sent him home to Hainan. Both Zheng and his wife reportedly were charged with "illegal business activity."

Forced relocation because of urban development continued and in some locations increased during the year. Protests over relocation terms or compensation were common, and some protest leaders were prosecuted. In rural areas infrastructure and commercial development projects resulted in the forced relocation of millions of persons.

Property-related disputes between citizens and government authorities, which often turned violent, were widespread in both urban and rural areas. These disputes frequently stemmed from local officials' collusion with property developers to pay little or no compensation to displaced residents, combined with a lack of effective government oversight or media scrutiny of local officials' involvement in property transactions, as well as a lack of legal remedies or other dispute resolution mechanisms for displaced residents. The problem persisted despite the central government's efforts to impose stronger controls over illegal land seizures and to standardize compensation. Redevelopment in traditional Uighur neighborhoods in cities throughout the XUAR, such as the Old City area in Kashgar, resulted in the destruction of historically or culturally important areas. Some residents voiced opposition to the lack of proper compensation provided by the government and coercive measures used to obtain their agreement to redevelopment. There were several reports of herders in Inner Mongolia complaining of confiscation of traditional pastoral lands for development.

Foreign media reported that at least 53 persons had self-immolated since 2009 to protest destruction of their homes.

For information on the government's family planning policies and their consequences, see section 6, Women.

SECTION 2. RESPECT FOR CIVIL LIBERTIES, INCLUDING

a. Freedom of Speech and Press

The law provides for freedom of speech and press, although authorities generally did not respect these rights. Authorities continued to control print, broadcast, and electronic media tightly and used them to propagate government views and CCP ideology. During the year authorities imposed censorship and manipulated the press and the internet, particularly around sensitive anniversaries.

Freedom of Speech: With significant exceptions, especially speech that challenged the government or the CCP, political topics could be discussed privately and in small groups without official punishment. During the year some independent think tanks, study groups, and seminars reported pressure to cancel some sessions on sensitive topics. Those who made politically sensitive comments in public speeches, academic discussions, and comments to the media remained subject to punitive measures.

In March the government merged the State Administration of Radio, Film, and Television with the General Administration of Press and Publication to create a new broadcast and press regulatory body, the General Administration of Press, Publication, Radio, Film, and Television.

On September 9, the Supreme People's Court and Supreme People's Procuratorate issued a judicial interpretation that made online rumormongering a punishable offense. Under the interpretation the author of a libelous internet post that is reposted more than 500 times or read more than 5,000 times, or of an internet post that led to mass protests, instigated ethnic or religious clashes, damaged the country's image or caused "a bad international effect," is subject to a maximum of three years in prison. By year's end this interpretation had a chilling effect on online discourse.

The government frequently monitored gatherings of intellectuals, scholars, and dissidents where political or sensitive issues were discussed. In 2008, to commemorate International Human Rights Day, a group of 303 intellectuals and activists released a petition entitled Charter '08, calling for the CCP to respect human rights and implement democratic reforms. Since then Charter '08 signers continued to report official harassment, especially around sensitive dates.

According to Western media reports, Shenzhen activist Yang Mingyu (also known as Yang Lin) was arrested July 19 for "inciting subversion of state power" in connection with his democracy activism, participation in Charter '08, and efforts to disclose official corruption.

On August 12, activist Liu Jiacai, who served two years administrative detention sentence on a charge of "inciting subversion of state power" in 2002, was detained in Hubei Province on criminal charges of "inciting subversion of state power." Police reported that he was detained for posting and disseminating online writings and views about legal reform in China. NGO sources reported that the charges stemmed from the fact that Liu had gathered activists in Yichang, Hubei Province for dinner parties, where they discussed corruption and other sensitive topics.

Press Freedoms: All books and magazines require state-issued publication numbers, which were expensive and often difficult to obtain. Nearly all print media, broadcast media, and book publishers were affiliated with the CCP or a government agency. There were a small number of print publications with some private ownership interest but no privately owned television or radio stations. The CCP directed the domestic media to refrain from reporting on certain subjects, and all broadcast programming required government approval.

In November the General Administration of Press, Publication, Radio, Film, and Television began requiring news organizations to hold weekly lectures on the CCP's journalistic principles, and journalists applying to renew their media credentials are required to take an examination on Marxist journalistic ideals.

Foreign journalists based in the country found a challenging environment for reporting. According to the annual "Reporting Conditions" survey of the Foreign Correspondents' Club of China (FCCC), "98 percent of respondents do not think reporting conditions in China meet international standards, and 70 percent feel conditions have worsened or stayed the same as the year before."

On July 8, journalist and documentary filmmaker Du Bin was released from a Beijing jail on bail after being detained for five weeks for allegedly "disturbing order at a public place." In May, Du had posted an online documentary about the Masanjia Women's RTL Camp in Liaoning Province (see section 1.c.), and also in May a publisher with offices in Hong Kong and New York published his book on the Tiananmen massacre.

Violence and Harassment: On July 15, law enforcement officers in Baita District of Liaoyang, Liaoning Province, allegedly beat a *Chinese Business Morning View* journalist who was reporting on a dispute between residents and developers at a construction site and destroyed his interview recordings.

Restrictions on foreign journalists by central and local CCP propaganda departments remained strict, especially during sensitive times and anniversaries. Foreign press outlets reported that local employees of foreign news agencies were also subject to official harassment and intimidation. During the year the FCCC "found 63 cases in which police officers or unknown persons impeded foreign reporters from doing their work, including nine cases in which reporters were manhandled or subjected to physical force." The report adds that while "this represents a welcome drop from last year," such intimidation "remains unacceptable."

According to Western media reports, in February a group of unidentified men in four vehicles assaulted a German television crew filming in a village near Beijing. According to a German correspondent present at the scene, the men ran the crew's minivan off the road and then smashed its windshield with baseball bats.

In December, Chinese authorities prevented a Western reporter from attending a press event with UK Prime Minister David Cameron and Chinese Prime Minister Li Keqiang.

The FCCC reported that, although routine delays in the provision of journalist visas appear to have shortened in recent months, 10 percent of survey respondents reported difficulties in obtaining official press accreditation or a journalist visa because of their reporting or that of their predecessors. While some reporters who authored particularly controversial news articles ultimately had their visas renewed, their news organizations experienced difficulty obtaining visas for new journalists and staff, even when these individuals previously held journalist visas for China.

Additionally, among the correspondents surveyed, 30 percent stated their Chinese assistants encountered pressure from officials or experienced harassment.

The government limited attendance at official press briefings to domestic media. Foreign media and diplomats were allowed to attend only briefings conducted by the Ministry of Foreign Affairs and a handful of press briefings held around special events.

Authorities continued to enforce tight restrictions on citizens employed by foreign news organizations. The code of conduct for Chinese employees of foreign media organizations threatens with dismissal and loss of accreditation Chinese employees who engage in "independent reporting" and instructs them to provide their employers information that projects a good image of the country.

Official guidelines for domestic journalists were often vague, subject to change at the discretion of propaganda officials, and enforced retroactively. Propaganda authorities forced newspapers to fire editors and journalists responsible for articles deemed inconsistent with official policy and suspended or closed publications. The system of postpublication review by propaganda officials encouraged self- censorship by editors seeking to avoid the losses associated with penalties for inadvertently printing unauthorized content. Officials can be punished for unauthorized contact with journalists.

Government officials used criminal prosecution, civil lawsuits, and other punishments, including violence, detention, and other forms of harassment, to intimidate authors and journalists and to prevent the dissemination of controversial writings. A domestic journalist can face demotion or job loss for publishing views that challenge the government.

In January a group of current and former journalists from the Guangzhou newspaper *Southern Weekend* (also translated as *Southern Weekly*), part of the *Nanfang Daily Group*, accused provincial propaganda officials of altering the newspaper's traditional New Year's message, which called for increased respect for constitutional rights. *Southern Weekend* journalists went on strike January 6 to protest editorial censorship, and students and activists began holding supportive demonstrations in front of the newspaper offices in Guangzhou. The protests turned into a broader public backlash against press censorship and were supported by editors, reporters, and social media. An agreement between the newspaper's staff and party overseers ended the strike January 8 and allowed the newspaper to resume publication January 10, but a clampdown on dissent reportedly followed. According to media reports, local authorities forcibly dispersed anticensorship protests, detained several activists for expressing solidarity with the newspaper, and blocked and deleted all references to the controversy from the internet.

Journalists who remained in prison at year's end included Yang Tongyan, and Dhondup Wangchen. Uighur webmasters Dilshat Perhat and Nijat Azat continued to serve sentences for "endangering state security." Uighur journalist Memetjan Abdulla was sentenced to life in prison in 2010, reportedly for transmitting "subversive" information related to the 2009 riots. During the year journalists working in traditional and new media were also imprisoned. In December 2012 the Prison Census of the Committee to Protect Journalists reported that, of 32 known journalists imprisoned in the country, 12 were ethnic Tibetan, seven were ethnic Uighur, and one was ethnic Mongolian. The committee documented two new imprisonment cases in 2012.

Censorship or Content Restrictions: Authorities continued to confiscate "unauthorized publications." According to the National Office Against Pornographic and Illegal Publications, 45 million illegal publications were confiscated and more than 3.7 million pieces of online information involving pornography or other illegal content were deleted in 2012.

Foreign journalists were denied permits to travel to the TAR, except for a very few highly controlled, government-organized press visits. Travel to Tibetan areas outside the TAR became increasingly difficult for foreign journalists. While foreign journalists were allowed access to Urumqi, XUAR, local and provincial authorities continued to control strictly the travel, access, and interviews of foreign journalists, even forcing them to leave cities in parts of the XUAR. After French news station France 24 broadcast journalist Cyril Payen's documentary about Tibet on May 30, Chinese embassy personnel went to the channel's headquarters in Paris to demand the withdrawal of the documentary from the station's website. The Chinese embassy in Bangkok also threatened Payen by telephone, according to Reporters Without Borders.

Media outlets received regular guidance on topics that should not be covered from the CCP's Central Propaganda Department. For example, in April the department issued censorship instructions to mainland media prohibiting them from reusing, reporting, and commenting on *Lens* magazine's April article on the Masanjia Women's Labor Re-education Camp in Liaoning Province (see section 1.c.).

Following an October typhoon in Yuyao, Zhejiang Province, that killed 10 persons and sparked protests about the government response, the State Council Information Office issued instructions to media outlets and internet companies not to report a local newspaper's story about the protests.

In December 2012 the Central Propaganda Department ordered media outlets to adhere strictly to the information provided by authoritative departments when reporting on officials suspected of involvement in graft or bribery. Throughout the year the Central Propaganda Department issued similar instructions regarding the election of Hong Kong's chief executive, the self-immolation of Tibetans, and the Bo Xilai scandal. The orders included instructions for media outlets not to investigate or report on their own.

Authorities continued to ban books with content they deemed controversial. The law permits only government-approved publishing houses to print books. The State Press and Publications Administration (PPA) controlled all licenses to publish. Newspapers, periodicals, books, audio and video recordings, or electronic publications may not be printed or distributed without the approval of the PPA and relevant provincial publishing authorities. Individuals who attempted to publish without government approval faced imprisonment, fines, confiscation of their books, and other sanctions. The CCP exerted control over the publishing industry by preemptively classifying certain topics as state secrets.

Many intellectuals and scholars exercised self-censorship, anticipating that books or papers on political topics would be deemed too sensitive to be published. The censorship process for private and government media also increasingly relied on self-censorship and, in a few cases, postpublication sanctions.

The General Administration of Press, Publication, Radio, Film, and Television, and the CCP remained active in issuing restrictive regulations and decisions constraining the content of broadcast media.

Authorities continued to jam, with varying degrees of success, Chinese-, Uighur-, and Tibetan-language broadcasts of the Voice of America (VOA), the BBC, and RFA. English-language broadcasts on the VOA generally were not jammed. Internet distribution of streaming radio news and podcasts from these sources often was blocked. Despite the jamming of overseas broadcasts, the VOA, the BBC, RFA, Deutsche Welle, and Radio France International had large audiences, including human rights advocates, ordinary citizens, and government officials.

Overseas television newscasts, largely restricted to hotels and foreign residence compounds, were occasionally subject to censorship. Such censorship of foreign broadcasts also occurred around the anniversary of the 1989 Tiananmen massacre and during the 18th Party Congress in 2012. Individual issues of foreign newspapers and magazines were occasionally banned when they contained articles deemed too sensitive. After two U.S. media websites published articles on *Bloomberg.com* and in the *New York Times* detailing the family wealth of Xi Jinping and Wen Jiabao, websites for both media outlets were blocked.

Politically sensitive coverage in Chinese, and to a lesser extent in English, were censored more than coverage in other languages. The government prohibited some foreign and domestic films deemed too sensitive or selectively censored parts of films before they were released.

Internet Freedom

In 2010 the Information Office of the State Council released its first White Paper on the internet outlining the government's endeavors to allow certain freedoms of speech on the internet as long as the speech did not endanger state security, subvert state power, damage state honor and interests, jeopardize state religious policy, propagate heretical or superstitious ideas, or spread rumors and other content forbidden by laws and administrative regulations, among other caveats. The internet was widely available and widely used. The China Internet Network Information Center (CNNIC) reported that by the end of 2012 the number of internet users reached 564 million, including 420 million mobile telephone internet users. The CNNIC reported that 50.9 million new users were added in 2012 – a 3.8 percent increase from 2011. The International Telecommunication Union reported that 39 percent of individuals used the internet and 41 percent of households had access to the internet by the end of the year.

The CCP underscored the importance of maintaining security and promoting core socialist values on the internet in its official decision adopted at the Sixth Plenum of the 17th CCP Congress in October 2011. The document called for developing a "healthy and uplifting network culture" that entails measures such as "step[ping] up guidance and management over social networks and instant messaging tools, standardiz[ing] the transmission order of information on the internet, and foster[ing] a civilized and rational network environment."

The CCP continued to increase efforts to monitor internet use, control content, restrict information, block access to foreign and domestic websites, encourage self- censorship, and punish those who ran afoul of political sensitivities. According to news sources, more than 14 government ministries participated in these efforts, resulting in the censorship of thousands of domestic and foreign websites, blogs, cell phone text messages, social networking services, online chat rooms, online games, and e-mail. These measures were not universally effective. In addition to its own extensive system of internet censorship, the government imposed more responsibilities on internet companies to implement online censorship and surveillance regimes, and it sought to prohibit anonymous expression online.

A State Council regulation deems personal blogs, computer bulletin boards, and cell phone text messages to be part of the news media, which subjects these media to state restrictions on content. Internet service providers were instructed to use only domestic media news postings, to record information useful for tracking users and their viewing habits, to install software capable of copying e-mails, and to end immediately transmission of "subversive material."

Under guidance from the CCP, the government employed thousands of persons at the national, provincial, and local levels to monitor electronic communications. Official monitoring focused on such tools as social networking, microblogging, and video-sharing sites. Internet companies also employed thousands of censors to implement CCP directives.

In 2011 central government authorities ordered all public spaces offering free wireless internet access to install costly software that would enable police to identify users of the service. Authorities warned Beijing cafe and restaurant owners they would face a fine of 20,000 renminbi (RMB) ($3,270) if they offered wireless internet access without installing the software. In December 2012 the NPC ratified a law requiring persons to give their real names when signing up for internet, fixed telephone line, or mobile telephone services. Providers must also require persons' names when allowing them to post information publicly.

Major news portals require users to register using their real names and identification numbers to comment on news articles. Individuals using the internet in public libraries are required to register using their national identity card, and usage reportedly was monitored at all public library terminals.

The government consistently blocked access to websites it deemed controversial, especially those discussing Taiwan, the Dalai Lama, Tibet, underground religious and spiritual organizations, democracy activists, and the 1989 Tiananmen massacre. The government also at times blocked access to selected sites operated by foreign governments, news outlets, health organizations, educational institutions, NGOs, and social networking sites, as well as to search engines that allow rapid communication or organization of users.

In June 2012, following the publication of an expose on the financial affairs of Xi Jinping's family, the government blocked access to a Western media website. In October 2012 the government blocked access to the English- and Chinese- language versions of a U.S. media website after it published an article on Wen Jiabao's family fortunes. At year's end, several Western media and social media websites were not accessible.

Some websites included images of cartoon police officers that warn users to stay away from forbidden content. Operators of web portals, blog-hosting services, and other content providers engaged in self-censorship to ensure their servers were free from politically sensitive content. Domestic websites that refused to self-censor political content were shut down, and many foreign websites were blocked. Millions of citizens had Twitter-like microblogs that circulated some news banned in the national media. The microblogs themselves were censored but often hours or days after the posting.

In July 2012 the State Internet Information Office and the State Administration of Radio, Film and Television issued a circular requiring online video content providers to review videos before making them available online and holding them responsible for the content.

Authorities employed an array of technical measures to block "sensitive" websites based in foreign countries. The ability of users to access such sensitive sites varied from city to city. The government also automatically censored e-mail and web chats based on a list of sensitive key words, such as "Falun Gong," "Dalai Lama," and "Tibetan independence." While such censorship was effective in keeping casual users away from sensitive content, it was defeated through the use of various technologies. Information on proxy servers outside China and software for defeating official censorship was readily available inside the country, but the government increasingly blocked access to the websites and proxy servers of commercial virtual private network providers. Despite official monitoring and censorship, dissidents and political activists continued to use the internet to call attention to political causes such as prisoner advocacy, political reform, ethnic discrimination, and corruption. Internet users spanning the political spectrum complained of censorship. Authorities sometimes blocked or closed the blogs of a number of prominent activists, artists, scholars, and university professors during the year.

There were numerous press reports of purported cyber-attacks against foreign websites, foreign journalists, and foreign media organizations that carried information deemed offensive by the government.

Authorities continued to jail numerous internet writers for peaceful expression of political views.

According to online reports, in June police in Fujian detained an online activist for 10 days for her microblog comments about a June 7 bus explosion in Xiamen. Police previously detained this same blogger in January 2012 for her comments about alleged corruption behind forced home evictions and demolitions in Xiamen's Jimei district.

The blog of environmental writer Liu Futang remained inaccessible. His blog, which exposed environmental problems caused by government-backed projects, was shut down in late 2012 after a Hainan Province court found him guilty of illegally profiting from self-published books.

The State Secrets Law obliges internet companies to cooperate with investigations of suspected leaks of state secrets, stop the transmission of such information once discovered, and report the crime to authorities. Furthermore, the companies must comply with authorities' orders to delete such information from their websites, and failure to do so is punishable by relevant departments such as the police and the Ministry of Public Security.

Regulations prohibit a broad range of activities that authorities interpret as subversive or slanderous to the state.

Academic Freedom and Cultural Events

The government continued restrictions on academic and artistic freedom, and political and social discourse at colleges, universities, and research institutes. The General Administration of Press, Publications, Radio, Film, and Television and the Central Propaganda Department issued restrictive regulations and decisions that constrained the flow of ideas and persons. In May the media reported that the CCP issued secret instructions to university faculty identifying seven "off-limits" subjects including universal values, freedom of the press, civil society, civil rights, an independent judiciary, elite cronyism, and the historical errors of the CCP. Some academics self-censored their publications, faced pressure to reach predetermined research results, or were unable to hold conferences with international participants during politically sensitive periods. Peking University economics professor Xia Yeliang came under government criticism for calling for public discussion of reform among intellectuals, and in October he was dismissed from his university position.

In December the East China University of Political Science and Law in Shanghai dismissed law professor Zhang Xuezhong for criticizing one-party rule in an online publication. According to reports, the school administration decided Zhang was unfit to teach after he refused to admit any wrongdoing.

Censorship and self-censorship of artistic works was common, particularly those artworks deemed to involve politically sensitive subjects.

Authorities on a few occasions blocked entry into the country of individuals deemed politically sensitive and declined to issue passports to Chinese citizens selected for international exchange programs who were considered "politically unreliable," singling out ethnic Tibetans and Uighurs and individuals from other minority nationality areas.

A number of other foreign government-sponsored exchange selectees, particularly those from minority provinces, encountered difficulties gaining approval to travel to participate in their programs.

The government used political attitudes and affiliations as criteria for selecting persons for the few government-sponsored study abroad programs but did not impose such restrictions on privately sponsored students. The government and the party controlled the appointment of high-level officials at universities. While CCP membership was not always a requirement to obtain a tenured faculty position, scholars without CCP affiliation often had fewer chances for promotion.

Foreign researchers, authors, and academics residing abroad reported they were subject to sanctions, including denial of visas, from authorities when their work did not meet with official approval. Thirteen foreign academics asserted that they were blacklisted and blocked from obtaining visas to travel to China for having contributed scholarly essays to a book on Xinjiang published in 2004. Other scholars continued to be blacklisted or faced difficulties obtaining visas because of their politically sensitive work on China.

b. Freedom of Peaceful Assembly and Association

Freedom of Assembly

While the law provides for freedom of peaceful assembly, the government severely restricted this right. The law stipulates that such activities may not challenge "party leadership" or infringe upon the "interests of the state." Protests against the political system or national leaders were prohibited. Authorities denied permits and quickly suppressed demonstrations involving expression of dissenting political views.

Citizens continued to gather publicly to protest evictions, relocations, and compensation in locations throughout the country, often resulting in conflict with authorities or other charges (see section 1.f.).

Guangdong police worked aggressively to curtail free speech and preempt peaceful assembly during the anniversary of the Tiananmen Square incident. Authorities ordered 15-day administrative detention for the organizers of one event. Police placed other activists under surveillance or house arrest, encouraged some to leave town on "vacation," or invited them to police stations for "tea" and questioning. Police also reportedly restricted the freedom of Foshan rights activist Chen Qitang and Guangzhou rights activists Wang

Aizhong and Tang Jingling in late May and early June in advance of and during the anniversary of the Tiananmen incident.

In January, Guangzhou police detained numerous persons involved in public demonstrations against the provincial propaganda department's censorship of *Southern Weekend*'s New Year's greeting. In addition to administrative detentions and formal arrests, police reportedly held a number of participants in irregular detention facilities including a movie theater and a military base (see section 2.a.).

On January 2, police in the Luoxi neighborhood of Guangzhou preemptively detained dozens of activists, including organizer Xu Lin, for planning a musical performance and poetry recitation at a public square to celebrate the New Year.

On February 23, Liu Yuandong, Sun Desheng, and 12 others were detained in Guangdong for their participation in protests directed at North Korea's nuclear test. Most of the protesters were freed or given administrative detentions, but police formally arrested and charged Liu on April 3. According to media reports, police subjected Liu and Sun to mistreatment in custody including sleep deprivation. On April 12, authorities in Dongguan, Guangdong Province, gave four activists administrative detentions after they held up banners calling for Liu's release. On August 13, authorities in Guangzhou again detained Sun Desheng for the crimes of gathering crowds and disrupting public order.

In May, Chengdu authorities preemptively deployed 170,000 security personnel throughout the city on the date of a planned protest against the construction of a nearby petrochemical plant and its production of paraxylene. Authorities also detained suspected activists in the days leading up to the planned protest.

Also in May, Changsha authorities in Hunan Province detained Xiang Yuhan following his organization of a peaceful march of 100 persons in commemoration of the International Day Against Homophobia. Xiang was confined for 12 days in administrative detention on a charge of "illegal protest."

In February the Nanjing NGO Tianxiagong (Justice for All) won a lawsuit against a hotel in Suzhou that in 2012 had canceled its conference reservations at the last moment on order from the local PSB. In May another NGO's legal rights conference in Hangzhou faced similar obstructions when hotels canceled reservations. The hotels informed the NGO that Zhejiang and Jiangsu province security officers ordered authorities not to permit holding the gathering anywhere in the provinces.

All concerts, sports events, exercise classes, or other meetings of more than 200 persons require approval from public security authorities. Although peaceful protests are legal, police rarely granted approval. Despite restrictions there were many demonstrations, but those with political or social themes were broken up quickly, sometimes with excessive force. The number of "mass incidents" and protests, including some violent protests, against local governments increased during the year. According to an international NGO, a former leading member of the CCP's Politics and Law Commission stated that the country experienced 30,000 to 50,000 mass incidents every year. As in past years, the vast majority of demonstrations concerned land disputes; housing problems; industrial, environmental, and labor matters; government corruption; taxation; and other economic and social concerns. Others were provoked by accidents or were related to personal petitions, administrative litigation, and other legal processes.

Disputes over land expropriation continued to trigger large-scale clashes between police and protesters.

The law protects an individual's ability to petition the government, but persons petitioning the government faced restrictions on their rights to assemble and raise grievances (see section 1.d.). Most petitions addressed grievances about land, housing, entitlements, the environment, or corruption. Most petitioners sought to present their complaints at national and provincial "letters and visits" offices.

Although banned by regulations, retaliation against petitioners reportedly continued. This was partly due to incentives the central government provided to local officials to prevent petitioners from raising complaints to higher levels. Incentives included provincial cadre evaluations based in part on the number of petitions from their provinces. This initiative aimed to encourage local and provincial officials to resolve legitimate complaints but also resulted in local officials sending security personnel to Beijing and forcibly returning the petitioners to their home provinces to prevent them from filing complaints against local officials with the central government. Such detentions often went unrecorded. Rules issued by the General Office of the State Council mandate sending officials from Beijing to the provinces to resolve petition problems locally, thereby reducing the number of petitioners entering Beijing. The rules also mandate a 60- day response time for petitions and provide for a single appeal in each case.

Petitioners faced harassment, illegal detention, and even more severe forms of punishment when attempting to travel to Beijing to present their grievances.

On January 5, authorities prevented 13 petitioners from Fujian Province from requesting assistance with their petitions from a foreign embassy in Beijing. According to online reports, police detained six of the petitioners for five days and one petitioner for 10 days.

Freedom of Association

The law provides for freedom of association, but the government restricted this right. CCP policy and government regulations require that all professional, social, and economic organizations officially register with, and receive approval from the government. These regulations prevented the formation of truly autonomous political, human rights, religious, spiritual, labor, and other organizations that the government believed might challenge its authority.

The government maintained tight controls over civil society organizations. According to regulations issued by the State Administration for Foreign Exchange, foreign exchange donations to or by domestic institutions must "comply with the laws and regulations...and shall not go against social morality or damage public interests and the legitimate rights and interests of other citizens." For donations to a domestic organization from a foreign NGO, the regulations require all parties and the banks to approve additional measures prior to processing a transaction. Application of the regulation varied, with some NGOs successfully navigating the requirements, others identifying other options by which to receive funds, and some severely limiting or shutting down operations.

To register, an NGO must find a government agency to serve as its organizational sponsor, have a registered office, and hold a minimum amount of funds. Some organizations with social or educational purposes that previously registered as private or for-profit businesses reportedly were requested to find a government sponsor and reregister as NGOs during the year. Finding a government sponsor was often very difficult, since the government department can be held responsible if the NGO engages in sensitive behavior. In March the NPC announced changes for NGO registration that waived the requirement to find a government sponsor. However, these changes only apply to four types of NGOs – industrial associations, charities, community services, and organizations dedicated to the promotion of technology. NGO sources reported that the new regulations do not apply to organizations primarily focused on advocacy or rights promotion.

In July the Ministry of Civil Affairs announced the intention to pass legislation that would allow international NGOs to register with provincial civil affairs authorities instead of the ministry. By year's end the legislation had not been promulgated.

In 2012 Guangdong provincial government officials initiated proposals aimed at facilitating the operations and work of many NGOs, including, for example, simplifying registration procedures so that certain categories of NGOs could register directly with the Ministry of Civil Affairs. Implementation of regulations associated with these proposals was often inconsistent. Although some NGOs perceived to be working in nonpolitically sensitive areas enjoyed increased opportunities, others continued to face interference from authorities, for example, through increased financial scrutiny. Labor NGOs in Shenzhen continued to face a challenging environment, including registration hurdles and occasional government interference with their activities.

Although registered organizations all came under some degree of government control, some NGOs were able to operate with a greater degree of independence.

The number of NGOs continued to grow, despite the restrictions and regulations. The government used the term "social organization" to categorize social groups (shehui tuanti), such as trade and professional associations; civil noncommercial units (minban fei qiye danwei), which are the equivalent of nonprofit service providers; and foundations (jijinhui). The last category included two types of foundations: public fundraising and private fundraising foundations. The government continued to impose fundraising limits on private foundations.

According to the Ministry of Civil Affairs, by the end of 2012 there were at least one million NGOs either operating without legal status or registered as companies. The country had approximately 462,000 legally registered social organizations, including 255,000 social groups, 204,000 civil noncommercial units, and 2,614 foundations. In 2012 an official of the Ministry of Civil Affairs wrote, "In 2007 China started to use the term 'social organization' instead of 'civil organization' because 'civil' contrasts with 'official' and reflected the opposing roles of civil society and government in the traditional political order. The 16th and 17th CCP Congresses changed the name to 'social organization.' NGOs existed under a variety of formal and informal guises, including national mass organizations created and funded by the CCP, known as 'government NGOs.'"

The lack of legal registration created numerous logistical challenges for NGOs, including difficulty opening bank accounts and receiving foreign funding, hiring workers, fundraising, and renting office space. NGOs that opted not to partner with government agencies could register as commercial consulting companies, which allowed them to obtain legal recognition at the cost of forgoing tax-free status. Security authorities routinely warned domestic NGOs, regardless of their registration status, not to accept donations from the foreign-funded National Endowment for Democracy and other international organizations deemed sensitive by the government.

In July officials from the Beijing Civil Affairs Bureau raided, closed, and confiscated materials from the think tank Transition Institute for not registering properly. The institute registered as a business, and its head, Guo Yushan, was associated with the New Citizens Movement and activists such as Chen Guangcheng and Xu Zhiyong.

Authorities supported the growth of some NGOs that focused on social problems such as poverty alleviation and disaster relief, but remained concerned that these organizations might emerge as a source of political opposition. NGOs working in the TAR and other Tibetan areas faced an increasingly difficult operating environment, and many were forced to curtail their activities altogether due to travel restrictions, official intimidation of staff members, and the failure of local partners to renew project agreements.

No laws or regulations specifically govern the formation of political parties. The Chinese Democracy Party remained banned, and the government continued to monitor, detain, and imprison current and former CDP members.

c. Freedom of Religion

See the Department of State's International Religious Freedom Report at www.state.

d. Freedom of Movement, Internally Displaced Persons, Protection of Refugees, and Stateless Persons

The law provides for freedom of internal movement, foreign travel, emigration, and repatriation, but the government generally did not respect these rights. While seriously restricting its scope of operations, the government occasionally cooperated with the Office of the UN High Commissioner for Refugees (UNHCR), which maintained an office in Beijing, to provide protection and assistance to refugees, asylum seekers, and other persons of concern.

Increasingly the government silenced activists by denying them permission to travel, both internationally and domestically, or keeping them under unofficial house arrest. In the spring officials denied Jiangsu environmental activist Wu Lihong a passport to travel abroad to accept a human rights award, although his wife and daughter were eventually permitted to travel and accepted the award on his behalf. Uighur economist Ilham Tohti was detained at Beijing airport and prevented from traveling abroad to accept a position as a visiting scholar.

In-country Movement: Authorities heightened restrictions on freedom of movement, particularly to curtail the movement of individuals deemed politically sensitive, before key anniversaries, visits by foreign dignitaries, or major political events and to forestall demonstrations. Freedom of movement continued to be very limited in the TAR and other Tibetan areas. Police maintained checkpoints in most counties and on roads leading into many towns, as well as within major cities such as Lhasa. Tibetans from other provinces reported that authorities subjected them to onerous documentation requirements to enter the TAR and required Tibetans who were not residents of Lhasa to obtain permission to enter the city, often forcing them to stay in specially designated accommodations, requirements not imposed on Han Chinese visitors to the TAR.

In 2012 prominent Tibetan poet and blogger Woeser, a Beijing resident, was required to leave Beijing and return to Lhasa for three months before and during the 18th Party Congress in Beijing. Uighur economics professor Ilham Tohti was also required to leave Beijing during the Party Congress. Feng Zhenghu, Mao Hengfeng, and other Shanghai activists reported being repeatedly detained upon arrival in Beijing when attempting to visit other activists or petition the national government.

Although the government maintained restrictions on the freedom to change one's workplace or residence, the national household registration system (hukou) continued to change, and the ability of most citizens to move within the country to work and live continued to expand. Rural residents continued to migrate to the cities, where the per capita disposable income was more than four times the rural per capita income, but many could not change their official residence or workplace within the country. Most cities had annual quotas for the number of new temporary residence permits that could be issued, and all workers, including university graduates, had to compete for a limited number of such permits. It was particularly difficult for rural residents to obtain household registration in more economically developed urban areas.

The household registration system added to the difficulties rural residents faced even after they relocated to urban areas and found employment. According to the 2012 Statistical Communique of the People's Republic of China on 2012 National *Economic and Social Development* published in February by the Ministry of Human Resources and Social Security, 279 million persons lived outside the jurisdiction of their household registration. Of that number, 236 million individuals worked outside their home district. Many migrant workers and their families faced numerous obstacles with regard to working conditions and labor rights. Many were unable to access public services, such as public education or social insurance, in the cities where they lived and worked because they were not legally registered urban residents. Poor treatment and difficulty integrating into local communities contributed to increased unrest among migrant workers in the Pearl River Delta. Migrant workers had little recourse when abused by employers and officials. Some major cities maintained programs to provide migrant workers and their children access to public education and other social services free of charge, but migrants in some locations reported difficulty in obtaining these benefits due to the onerous bureaucratic processes involved in obtaining access to urban services.

Under the "staying at prison employment" system applicable to recidivists incarcerated in RTL camps, authorities denied certain persons permission to return to their homes after serving their sentences. Some released or paroled prisoners returned home but were not permitted freedom of movement.

Foreign Travel: The government permitted legal emigration and foreign travel for most citizens. Some academics and activists continued to face travel restrictions, especially around sensitive anniversaries (see section 1.d.). The government exercised exit control for departing passengers at airports and other border crossings and utilized this exit control to deny foreign travel to dissidents and persons employed in sensitive government posts. Throughout the year lawyers, artists, authors, and other activists were at times prevented from freely exiting the country. Border officials and police cited threats to "national security" as the reason for refusing permission to leave the country. Authorities stopped most persons at the airport at the time of the attempted travel. Wuxi environmental activist Wu Lihong was prevented from traveling abroad to accept a human rights award in July. Shanghai activist Zheng Enchong was prevented from accepting a teaching fellowship in Hong Kong in August. Shanghai activist Chen Jianfang was prevented from traveling to a UN human rights training course in Geneva in September. Well known artist Ai

Weiwei was denied a passport to attend exhibitions of his work abroad. Other activists also reported being blocked from traveling abroad.

Most citizens could obtain passports, although those government deemed potential threats, including religious leaders, political dissidents, petitioners, and ethnic minorities, reported routinely being refused passports or otherwise prevented from traveling overseas.

Ethnic Uighurs, particularly those residing in the XUAR, reported that it was very difficult to get a passport application approved at the local level. They were frequently denied passports to travel abroad, particularly to Saudi Arabia for the haj, other Muslim countries, or Western countries for academic or other purposes. Authorities reportedly seized valid passports of some residents of the XUAR and other citizens.

In the TAR and Tibetan areas of Qinghai, Gansu, and Sichuan provinces, ethnic Tibetans experienced great difficulty acquiring passports. The unwillingness of Chinese authorities in Tibetan areas to issue or renew passports for ethnic Tibetans created, in effect, a ban on foreign travel for a large segment of the Tibetan population. Han residents of Tibetan areas did not experience the same difficulties.

Authorities denied Tibetan blogger and poet Woeser's passport application, preventing her from receiving the Secretary of State's International Women of Courage award in person. According to an RFA report, in June authorities placed Woeser and her husband under house arrest for speaking up about conditions in Tibet ahead of a state-sponsored trip by foreign journalists to the TAR.

Exile: The law neither provides for a citizen's right to repatriate nor addresses exile. The government continued to refuse reentry to numerous Chinese citizens who were considered dissidents, Falun Gong activists, or "troublemakers." Although authorities allowed some dissidents living abroad to return, dissidents released on medical parole and allowed to leave the country often were effectively exiled. Authorities imprisoned some activists residing abroad upon their return to the country.

Emigration and Repatriation: The government continued to try to prevent many Tibetans and Uighurs from leaving the country and detained many who were apprehended in flight. During the year 171 Tibetans transited the UNHCR reception center in Kathmandu. There also were reports of the forcible return of Uighur asylum seekers from Malaysia in 2012. Of a group of 20 Uighurs returned from Cambodia in 2009, three persons, a woman and two children, were reportedly freed, and in 2011, 16 others received prison sentences ranging from 16 years to life. Chinese authorities continued to refuse to provide information regarding the whereabouts of the remaining individual.

Protection of Refugees

Access to Asylum: The law does not provide for the granting of refugee or asylee status, and the government did not establish a system for providing protection to refugees. Although the government does not grant refugee or asylee status, it allowed the UNHCR more latitude in assisting non-North Korean and non- Burmese refugees. The UNHCR office in Beijing recognized approximately 100 refugees from Pakistan, Iraq, Somalia, and Eritrea and was processing approximately 100 additional individuals who requested refugee status. Because the PRC did not officially recognize these individuals as refugees, they remained in the country as illegal immigrants unable to work, with no access to education, and subject to deportation at any time.

Refoulement: The government did not provide protection against the expulsion or forcible return of vulnerable refugees and asylum seekers, especially North Korean and Kachin refugees, to countries where their lives or freedom would be threatened on account of their race, religion, nationality, membership in a particular social group, or political opinion. The government continued to consider all North Koreans "economic migrants" rather than refugees or asylum seekers, and the UNHCR continued to have no access to North Korean or Burmese refugees inside China. The lack of access to durable solutions and options, as well as constant fear of forced repatriation by authorities, left North Korean refugees vulnerable to human traffickers. Reports of various exploitation schemes targeting North Korean refugees, such as forced marriages, forced labor, and prostitution, were common. The government continued to deny the UNHCR permission to operate along its borders with North Korea and Burma.

Some North Koreans who entered diplomatic compounds in the country were permitted to travel to foreign countries after waiting for periods of up to two years.

On May 27, there were reports that the government of Laos coordinated with the Democratic People's Republic of Korea (DPRK) to deport nine North Korean asylum seekers from Laos to China. On June 3, the Foreign Ministry spokesperson stated the nine individuals entered China on May 27 and subsequently left Beijing bound for the DPRK holding valid travel documents and visas.

After two-time North Korean defector and South Korean citizen Kim Kwang-ho defected from North Korea to China for the second time, Chinese security officials in Yanji, Jilin Province, detained Kim, his wife Kim Ok-sil, and their daughter in July and held them until August before allowing them to return to South Korea. Chinese authorities reportedly repatriated to North Korea Kim's North Korean brother- and sister-in-law, who defected with him.

Refugee Abuse: The intensified crackdown begun in 2008 against North Korean asylum seekers and refugees reportedly extended to harassment of religious communities along the border. The government arrested and detained individuals who provided food, shelter, transportation, and other assistance to North Koreans. According to reports some activists or brokers detained for assisting North Koreans were charged with human smuggling, and in some cases the North Koreans were forcibly returned. There were also reports that North Korean agents operated clandestinely within the country to repatriate North Korean citizens forcibly. According to press reports, some North Koreans detained by Chinese police faced repatriation unless they could pay bribes to secure their release.

Access to Basic Services: Undocumented children of some North Korean asylum seekers and of mixed couples (i.e., one Chinese parent and one North Korean parent) did not have access to health care, public education, or other social services due to lack of legal status.

Durable Solutions: The government largely cooperated with the UNHCR when dealing with the resettlement of ethnic Han Chinese or ethnic minorities from Vietnam and Laos who resided in the country since the Vietnam War era. During the year the government and the UNHCR continued discussions concerning the granting of citizenship to these long-term residents and their children, many of whom were born in China.

SECTION 3. RESPECT FOR POLITICAL RIGHTS: THE RIGHT OF CITIZENS TO CHANGE THEIR GOVERNMENT

The constitution states that "all power in the People's Republic of China belongs to the people" and that the organs through which the people exercise state power are the NPC and the people's congresses at provincial, district, and local levels. While the law provides citizens the right to change their government peacefully, citizens cannot freely choose or change the laws or officials that govern them. In fact the CCP controlled virtually all elections and continued to control appointments to positions of political power.

Elections and Political Participation

Recent Elections: The NPC, composed of up to 3,000 deputies, elects the president and vice president, the premier and vice premiers, and the chairman of the State Central Military Commission. The NPC Standing Committee, which consisted of 175 members, oversaw these elections and determined the agenda and procedures for the NPC.

The NPC Standing Committee remained under the direct authority of the CCP, and most legislative decisions require the concurrence of the CCP's seven-member Politburo Standing Committee. Despite its broad authority under the state constitution, the NPC did not set policy independently or remove political leaders without the CCP's approval.

According to Ministry of Civil Affairs statistics, almost all of the country's more than 600,000 villages had implemented direct elections for members of local subgovernmental organizations known as village committees. The direct election of officials by ordinary citizens remained narrow in scope and strictly confined to the local level. The government estimated that serious procedural flaws marred one-third of all elections. Corruption, vote buying, and interference by township- level and CCP officials continued to be problems. The law permits each voter to cast proxy votes for up to three other voters.

The election law governs legislative bodies at all levels, although compliance and enforcement was uneven across the country. Under this law citizens have the opportunity every five years to vote for local people's congress representatives at the county level and below, although in most cases higher-level government officials or CCP cadres controlled the nomination of candidates in those elections. At higher levels legislators selected people's congress delegates from among their ranks. For example, provincial-level people's congresses selected delegates to the NPC. Local CCP secretaries generally served concurrently within the leadership team of the local people's congress, thus strengthening CCP control over legislatures.

In 2012 the local governments kept most independent candidates – those without official government backing – off the ballots despite their meeting nomination criteria. No declared independent candidates won election in 2012. Election officials pressured independent candidates to renounce their candidacies, manipulated the ballot to exclude independent candidates, refused to disclose electorate information to independent candidates, and sometimes adjusted electoral districts to dilute voter support for independent candidates.

In September an independent People's Congress candidate from Foshan City, Guangdong Province, who was detained in 2011 during the People's

Congress representative elections that year on a charge of undermining elections, was tried and found guilty of "disrupting elections." According to open source websites, hundreds of her supporters who wanted to observe her trial were denied access to the court.

Political Parties: Official statements asserted, "The political party system [that] China has adopted is multi-party cooperation and political consultation under" CCP leadership. The CCP, however, retained a monopoly on political power, and the government forbade the creation of new political parties. The government officially recognized nine parties founded prior to 1949, and parties other than the CCP held 30 percent of the seats in the NPC. Activists attempting to support unofficial parties were arrested, detained, or confined.

In 2009 in Hunan Province, dissident Xie Changfa, who tried to organize a national meeting of the banned CDP, was sentenced to 13 years in prison. Guo Quan, a former Nanjing University professor and founder of the China New Democracy Party, remained imprisoned following his 2009 sentence to 10 years in prison and three years' deprivation of political rights for "subversion of state power." Guo published articles criticizing the country's one-party system. Other current or former CDP members, including Yang Tianshui, remained in prison or in RTL camps for their calls for political reform and their affiliation with the CDP.

Participation of Women and Minorities: While the government placed no special restrictions on the participation of women or minority groups in the political process, women held few positions of significant influence in the CCP or government structure. Among the 2,987 delegates of the 11th NPC (term 2008-13), 637 were women (21 percent).

Ten women occupied ministerial or higher-ranked positions.

According to government-provided information, there were more than 230 female provincial and ministerial officials, 10 percent of the overall total; 670 female mayors and vice mayors, twice the number from 1995; and one provincial governor, Li Bin in Anhui Province (until June). A total of 37 women were members of provincial standing committees, constituting 9 percent of standing committee members. Following the 18th Party Congress in November, two women were members of the CCP's 25-member Politburo. There were no women in the Standing Committee of the Politburo. There were approximately 15 million female CCP cadres, approximately one-fifth of the party's membership.

The government encouraged women to exercise their right to vote in village committee elections and to run in those elections, although only a small fraction of elected members were women. In many locations a seat on the village committee was reserved for a woman, who was usually given responsibility for family planning. The election law provides a general mandate for quotas for female and ethnic minority representatives, but achieving these quotas often required election authorities to violate the election procedures specified in the election law. During the 2011-12 local people's congresses elections, many electoral districts in which independent candidates campaigned used these quotas as justification to thwart the independent candidacies.

A total of 411 delegates from 55 ethnic minorities were members of 11th NPC, accounting for 14 percent of the total number of delegates. All of the country's officially recognized minority groups were represented.

The 18th Communist Party Congress elected 10 members of ethnic minority groups as members of the Central Committee.

The only ministerial-level post held by an ethnic minority member was in the State Ethnic Affairs Commission, headed by Yang Jing, an ethnic Mongol from Inner Mongolia. Until November 2012 Hui Liangyu of the Hui ethnic group was a member of the Politburo. Minorities held few senior CCP or government positions of significant influence (see also section 6, National/Racial/Ethnic Minorities).

SECTION 4. CORRUPTION AND LACK OF TRANSPARENCY IN GOVERNMENT

Although according to the law officials face criminal penalties for corruption, the government did not implement the law effectively, and officials frequently engaged in corrupt practices with impunity. Many cases of corruption involved areas heavily regulated by the government, such as land-usage rights, real estate, and infrastructure development, which were susceptible to fraud, bribery, and kickbacks. Court judgments often could not be enforced against powerful special entities, including government departments, state-owned enterprises, military personnel, and some members of the CCP.

While corruption remained a serious problem, there were increasing indications that the government recognized the seriousness of the problem.

In January the Central Commission for Discipline Inspection (CCDI), the CCP's leading body for countering corruption among members, reported that it had investigated 155,144 corruption-related cases and closed 153,704 of them and that the CCP and government had disciplined 160,718 officials.

In October the Supreme People's Procuratorate reported that prosecutors nationwide had investigated 18,283 cases involving bribery and major embezzlement from January to August. Among the suspects were 129 officials at the director general level and above.

In December the CCP Central Committee unveiled a five-year plan to punish and prevent corruption. On December 26, the CCDI reported it had punished 25,855 individuals for breaches to antibureaucracy and formalism rules during the year, including 6,247 CCP officials.

In February 2012 the NPC's Standing Committee amended the criminal law to make citizens and companies paying bribes to foreign government officials and officials of international public organizations subject to criminal punishments of up to 10 years' imprisonment and a fine.

In October 2012 the government established a "frugal working style" rule barring government officials from spending public money on luxury items such as lavish banquets and luxury cars and from accepting expensive gifts. In September the government banned officials from using public money to send mooncakes as gifts and in December published regulations that banned dishes containing shark fin, bird nests, and wild animal products from official banquets. In December the government issued guidelines forbidding officials from chartering planes or flying in private or corporate jets overseas.

In 2012 the Supreme People's Court urged local courts to ban family members of officials and judges from being lawyers under the local court's jurisdiction. Also in 2012 the Higher People's Court of Fujian Province forbade judges from meeting privately with representatives in a case.

In February 2012 the Supreme People's Procuratorate announced the availability of a national bribery database listing individuals and companies found guilty of certain offenses, including bribing an individual or entity, and facilitating bribery. Companies and individuals must apply in writing to have the procuratorate check nationwide to determine whether a particular individual or company has been convicted of bribery offenses in the PRC. Companies must provide a copy of their business license.

In June 2012 the Supreme People's Procuratorate stated it would strengthen measures to recover and freeze illegal assets transferred abroad by corrupt officials.

Corruption: In numerous cases during the year, public officials and leaders of state-owned enterprises, who generally hold high CCP ranks, were investigated for corruption. In June the CCDI announced that Guo Yongxiang, a former deputy governor of Sichuan Province, was under investigation for suspected disciplinary violations.

In July a Beijing court sentenced former railroads minister Liu Zhijun to death, with a two-year reprieve. Liu came under scrutiny for his mismanagement of the country's high-speed train network.

On August 26, the Ministry of Supervision announced that Wang Yongchun, a vice president at state-owned China National Petroleum Corporation and the general manager of Daqing oilfield in Heilongjiang Province, was being investigated for "severe disciplinary violations."

In September the Beijing Municipal People's Procuratorate confirmed that it had indicted former Jilin vice governor Tian Xueren on corruption charges but did not provide a trial date or information about the specific charges against him. Tian was reported to have been stripped of both his party membership and government position for taking bribes.

In December the CCDI investigated Vice-Minister of Public Security Li Dongsheng for "suspected serious law and discipline violations."

Notable organizations that worked to address official corruption included the Central Commission for Discipline Inspection, the Ministry of Supervision, the National Bureau of Corruption Prevention, the International Association of Anti- Corruption Authorities, and the Anti-Corruption and Governance Research Center at Tsinghua University.

Whistleblower Protection: In 1991 the Supreme People's Procuratorate published the Regulation to Protect Citizen's Whistleblowing Rights. Whistleblowing protections are also included in various criminal and labor laws. Legal experts opined, however, that the constellation of laws and regulations did not provide adequate protections to whistleblowers. In September the government created an official website for citizens to report fraud, graft, and government mismanagement, with priority given to those who provide their real names and contact information. The government does not provide legal protection for whistleblowers who do not use official channels.

Financial Disclosure: A 2010 regulation requires officials in government agencies or state-owned enterprises at the county level or above to report their ownership of property, including that in their spouses' or children's names, as well as their families' investments in financial assets and enterprises. According to Article 23 of the regulations, the monitoring bodies are the CCDI, the Organization Department of the CCP, and the Ministry of Supervision. The regulations do not state that declarations are to be made public. Instead, they are to go to a higher administrative level and a human resource department. Punishments for not declaring information vary from education on the regulations, warning talks, and adjusting one's work position to being relieved of one's position. Regulations further state that officials should report all income, including allowances, subsidies and bonuses, as well as income from other jobs such as giving lectures, writing, consulting, reviewing articles, painting, and calligraphy. Officials, their spouses, and the children who live with them also should report their real estate properties and financial investments. Government officials should report their marriage status, records of private travel abroad, marriage status of their children, and whether their spouses are from Hong Kong, Taiwan, or a foreign country. They must report whether their children live abroad, as well as the work status of their children and grandchildren (including those who live abroad). Officials are required to file reports annually and must report changes of personal status within 30 days.

In December 2012 officials announced that Guangdong Province would pilot a program in select districts requiring all CCP and government officials to report their assets publicly, with officials who refuse to do so to be relieved of their posts and subjected to further investigations. This program was not put into practice by year's end.

Public Access to Information: Open-government information regulations allow citizens to request information from the government. The regulations require government authorities to create formal channels for information requests and to include an appeal process if requests are rejected or not answered. They stipulate that administrative agencies should reply to requests immediately to the extent possible. Otherwise, the administrative agency should provide the information within 15 working days, with the possibility of a maximum extension of an additional 15 days. In cases in which third-party rights and interests are involved, the time needed to consult the third party does not count against the time limits. According to the regulations, administrative agencies may collect only cost-based fees (as determined by the State Council) for searching, photocopying, postage, and similar expenses when disclosing government information on request. Citizens requesting information can also apply for a fee reduction or exemption. The regulations include exceptions for state secrets, commercial secrets, and individual privacy.

Publicly released provincial- and national-level statistics for open-government information requests showed wide disparities across localities, levels of government, and departments in numbers of requests filed and official documents released in response.

If information requestors believe that an administrative agency has violated the regulations, they can report it to the next higher-level administrative agency, the supervision agency, or the department in charge of open-government information. In 2011 the Supreme People's Court ruled that citizens can sue any government department that refused to provide unclassified information. Shortly thereafter a Tsinghua University graduate student sued three government ministries after her requests for information regarding the duties of 14 ministries for use in her thesis were denied. A court delayed consideration of her case pending further research, and she withdrew her lawsuit after the ministries provided the requested information.

SECTION 5. GOVERNMENTAL ATTITUDE REGARDING INTERNATIONAL AND NONGOVERNMENTAL INVESTIGATION OF ALLEGED VIOLATIONS OF HUMAN RIGHTS

The government sought to maintain control over civil society groups, halt the emergence of independent NGOs, hinder the activities of civil society and rights' activist groups, and prevent what it called the "Westernization" of the country. The government did not permit independent domestic NGOs to monitor openly or to comment on human rights conditions, and it harassed domestic NGOs. The government tended to be suspicious of independent organizations and scrutinized NGOs with financial and other links overseas. Most large NGOs were quasi- governmental, and many official NGOs had to be sponsored by government agencies. The NPC introduced new registration procedures in March that allowed certain types of nonadvocacy NGOs to register directly with the Ministry of Civil Affairs (see section 2.b., Freedom of Association).

An informal network of activists around the country continued to serve as a credible source of information about human rights violations. The information was disseminated through organizations such as the Hong Kong-based Information Center for Human Rights and Democracy, the foreign-based Human Rights in China, and Chinese Human Rights Defenders and via the internet.

The government remained reluctant to accept criticism of its human rights record by other nations or international organizations. It criticized reports by international human rights monitoring groups, claiming that such reports were inaccurate and interfered with the country's internal affairs. Representatives of some international human rights organizations reported that authorities denied their visa requests or restricted the length of visas issued to them. The government continued to participate in official diplomatic human rights dialogues with foreign governments although some governments encountered problems scheduling such dialogues.

Government Human Rights Bodies: The government did not have a human rights ombudsman or commission. The government-established China Society for Human Rights was an NGO whose mandate is to defend the government's human rights record. The government maintained that each country's economic, social, cultural, and historical conditions influenced its approach to human rights.

SECTION 6. DISCRIMINATION, SOCIETAL ABUSES, AND TRAFFICKING IN PERSONS

While there were laws designed to protect women, children, persons with disabilities, and minorities, some discrimination based on ethnicity, sex, disability, and other factors persisted.

Women

Rape and Domestic Violence: Rape is illegal, and some persons convicted of rape were executed. The penalties for rape can range from three years in prison to a death sentence with a two-year reprieve and forced labor. The law does not address spousal rape. The government did not make available official statistics on rape or sexual assault, leaving the scale of sexual violence difficult to determine. Migrant female workers were particularly vulnerable to sexual violence.

Violence against women remained a significant problem. According to reports at least a quarter of families suffered from domestic violence, and more than 85 percent of the victims were women. Domestic violence against women included verbal and psychological abuse, restrictions on personal freedom, economic control, physical violence, and rape. The government supported shelters for victims of domestic violence, and some courts provided protections to victims, including through restraining orders prohibiting a perpetrator of domestic violence from coming near a victim. In March, Shaanxi Province designated the Number Two People's Hospital as an antidomestic violence service station to treat victims of domestic violence, the first designation of its kind. Nonetheless, official assistance did not always reach victims, and public security forces often ignored domestic violence. In 2010 the All China Women's Federation (ACWF) reported that it received 50,000 domestic violence complaints annually. Spousal abuse typically went unreported, and an ACWF study found that only 7 percent of rural women who suffered domestic violence sought help from police. Almost 30 percent of respondents in a recent study felt that domestic violence should be kept a private matter.

While domestic violence tended to be more prevalent in rural areas, it also occurred among the highly educated urban population. The ACWF reported that approximately one-quarter of the 400,000 divorces registered each year were the result of family violence.

According to ACWF statistics nationwide in 2008 there were 12,000 special police booths for domestic violence complaints, 400 shelters for victims of domestic violence, and 350 examination centers for women claiming injuries from domestic violence. Many domestic violence shelters had inadequate facilities, required extensive documentation, or went unused. The government operated most shelters, some with NGO participation. In 2012 the government provided 680,000 office spaces in government buildings for women's resource centers.

There was no strong legal mechanism to protect women from domestic abuse. According to the ACWF, laws related to domestic violence were flawed since there was no national provision for dealing with offenders. During the year the creation of such mechanisms was added to the NPC's legislative agenda, the fifth time the ACWF submitted such a proposal. Both the marriage law and the law on the protection of women's rights and interests have stipulations that directly prohibit domestic violence, but some experts complained that the stipulations were too general, failed to define domestic violence, and were difficult to implement. Because of standards of evidence, even if certain that domestic violence was occurring, a judge could not rule against the abuser without the abuser's confession. Only 10 percent of accused abusers confessed to violent behavior, according to 2009 data from the Institute of Applied Laws. The institute reported that, although 40 to 60 percent of marriage and family cases involved domestic violence, less than 30 percent were able to supply indirect evidence, including photographs, hospital records, police records, or children's testimony. Witnesses seldom testified in court.

Public support increased in the fight against domestic violence. A recent survey found that more than 85 percent of respondents believed that further antidomestic violence legislation was needed. A high-profile case, Kim Lee's case against her celebrity husband, Li Yang, led to public outcry when she posted pictures of her injuries on a social networking site. After months of waiting, Lee was granted a civil protection order forbidding her husband from approaching within 200 yards of her. In February a Beijing court granted Lee a divorce on the grounds of domestic abuse and issued a three-month protection order against her former husband. This case set a precedent because the court acknowledged domestic violence as grounds for divorce, granted a protection order, and ordered the former husband to pay compensation for the violence she had endured during their marriage.

Sexual Harassment: The law bans sexual harassment, and the number of sexual harassment complaints increased significantly. A 2009 Harvard University study showed that 80 percent of working women in the country experienced sexual harassment at some stage of their careers. The same study found that only 30 percent of sexual harassment claims by women achieved favorable resolutions. In November an NGO published its survey of female manufacturing workers in Guangzhou, which indicated that as much as 70 percent of Guangzhou's female workforce had been sexually harassed. Approximately half did not pursue legal or administrative actions, while 15 percent of respondents reported leaving the workplace to escape their harasser.

Sexual harassment was not limited to the workplace. According to a *China Youth Daily* survey reported in September, approximately 14 percent of women had been sexually harassed while riding the subway, and 82 percent of those polled believed the problem existed. At a Hainan Province festival in 2012, a dozen women were pinned down by a crowd of men who mauled the women and stripped off their clothes in broad daylight. Police escorted the women away and, according to press reports, subsequently detained six suspects in the assault.

According to information on the ACWF website, the internet and hotlines made it easier for women who were sexually harassed to obtain useful information and legal service. A Beijing rights lawyer told the ACWF that approximately 100-200 million women in the country had suffered or were suffering sexual harassment in the workplace but that very few legal service centers provided counseling.

Reproductive Rights: The government restricted the rights of parents to choose the number of children they have. Although national law prohibits the use of physical coercion to compel persons to submit to abortion or sterilization, intense pressure to meet birth-limitation targets set by government regulations resulted in instances of local family-planning officials' using physical coercion to meet government goals. Such practices included the mandatory use of birth control and the abortion of unauthorized pregnancies. In the case of families that already had two children, one parent was often pressured to undergo sterilization.

The National Population and Family Planning Commission reported that 13 million women annually underwent abortions caused by unplanned pregnancies. An official news media outlet also reported at least an additional 10 million chemically induced abortions or abortions performed in nongovernment facilities. Government statistics on the percentage of all abortions that were nonelective was not available. According to Health Ministry data released in March 2012, a total of 336 million abortions and 222 million sterilizations had been carried out since 1971.

The national family-planning authorities shifted their emphasis from lowering fertility rates to maintaining low fertility rates and emphasized quality of care in family-planning practices. In 2010 a representative of the National Population and Family Planning Commission reported that 85 percent of women of childbearing age used contraception. Of those, 70 percent used a reversible method. A survey taken in September, however, found that only 12 percent of women between the ages of 20 and 35 had a proper understanding of contraceptive methods. The country's birth-limitation policies retained harshly coercive elements in law and practice. The financial and administrative penalties for unauthorized births were strict.

The 2002 national population and family-planning law standardized the implementation of the government's birth-limitation policies, although enforcement varied significantly. The law grants married couples the right to have one birth and allows couples to apply for permission to have a second child if they meet conditions stipulated in local and provincial regulations. The one-child limit was more strictly applied in urban areas, where only couples meeting certain conditions were permitted to have a second child (e.g., if both of the would-be parents were an only child). In most rural areas couples were permitted to have a second child in cases where their first child was a girl. Ethnic minorities were subject to less stringent rules. Nationwide 35 percent of families fell under the one-child restrictions, and more than 60 percent of families were eligible to have a second child, either outright or if they met certain criteria. The remaining 5 percent were eligible to have more than two children. According to government statistics, the average fertility rate for women nationwide was 1.8, and in the country's most populous and prosperous city, Shanghai, the fertility rate was 0.8. In December the NPC Standing Committee amended the one-child policy to allow couples in which at least one spouse is an only child to have two children.

The National Population and Family Planning Commission reported that all provinces eliminated the birth-approval requirement before a first child is conceived, but provinces may still continue to require parents to "register" pregnancies prior to giving birth to their first child. This registration requirement could be used as a de facto permit system in some provinces, since some local governments continued to mandate abortion for single women who became pregnant. Provinces and localities imposed fines of various amounts on unwed mothers.

Regulations requiring women who violate family-planning policy to terminate their pregnancies still exist in Liaoning and Heilongjiang provinces. Other provinces – Fujian, Guizhou, Guangdong, Gansu, Jiangxi, Qinghai, Shanxi, and Shaanxi – require unspecified "remedial measures" to deal with unauthorized pregnancies. A number of online media reports indicated that migrant women applying for household registration in Guangzhou were required to have an intrauterine contraceptive device (IUD) implanted.

In October, Western media reported that officials from the Shandong Province Family Planning Commission forced their way into the home of Liu Xinwen, dragged her to a nearby hospital, and injected her with an abortion-inducing drug. Shandong officials reportedly forced Liu, who was six months into her pregnancy, to sign a document stating that she had agreed to the abortion.

The government continued to impose "child-raising fees" on violators of the one- child policy. In the first half of the year, for example, Guangzhou City collected more than RMB 300 million ($49 million) in such fees without disclosing how the money was used. Guangdong Province reportedly refused to disclose the amount of fees it had collected from one-child policy violators. Family planning officials in Tunchang County, Hainan Province, used fines and terminated employment as punishment for one-child policy violators.

On December 30, overseas media reported that officials at Nurluq Hospital in Keriye County of Xinjiang's Hotan Prefecture carried out forced abortions on four pregnant women. According to the report, the deputy chief of Hotan's Arish Township confirmed that authorities had carried out four of six planned abortions utilizing abortion-inducing drugs. One woman escaped and another was in the hospital awaiting the procedure, the report stated. The head of the township's Family Planning Department stated the abortions were carried out following orders from higher authorities. The husband of one victim stated that his wife had been seven months' pregnant when the procedure was performed and that the baby had been born alive before succumbing to the effects of the chemical toxins hours later.

The law requires each parent of an unapproved child to pay a "social compensation fee," which can reach 10 times a person's annual disposable income.

Social compensation fees were set and assessed at the local level. The law requires family-planning officials to obtain court approval before taking "forcible" action, such as detaining family members or confiscating and destroying property of families who refuse to pay social compensation fees. This requirement was not always followed, and national authorities remained ineffective at reducing abuses by local officials.

The population control policy relied on education, propaganda, and economic incentives, as well as on more coercive measures. Those who had an unapproved child or helped another do so faced disciplinary measures such as social compensation fees, job loss or demotion, loss of promotion opportunity, expulsion from the CCP (membership is an unofficial requirement for certain jobs), and other administrative punishments, including in some cases the destruction of private property.

It continued to be illegal in almost all provinces for a single woman to have a child, with fines levied for violations. The law states that family-planning bureaus conduct pregnancy tests on married women and provide them with unspecified "follow-up" services. Some provinces fined women who did not undergo periodic pregnancy tests.

Officials at all levels remained subject to rewards or penalties based on meeting the population goals set by their administrative region. Promotions for local officials depended in part on meeting population targets. Linking job promotion with an official's ability to meet or exceed such targets provided a powerful structural incentive for officials to employ coercive measures to meet population goals. An administrative reform process initiated pilot programs in some localities that removed this criterion for evaluating officials' performance.

Although the family-planning law states that officials should not violate citizens' rights in the enforcement of family-planning policy, these rights, as well as penalties for violating them, are not clearly defined. By law citizens may sue officials who exceed their authority in implementing birth-planning policy, but few protections for whistleblowers against retaliation from local officials exist (see section 4, Whistleblower Protection). The law provides significant and detailed sanctions for officials who help persons evade the birth limitations.

According to online reports, women who registered newborns in Nanhai District, Foshan, Guangdong Province, were requested to insert an IUD. Many posted online complaints that officials threatened not to register the baby if the mother did not comply, even when the newborn was the mother's only child. Other reports indicated that a mother could not enroll her child in school if she was unwilling to insert an IUD.

Discrimination: The constitution states that "women enjoy equal rights with men in all spheres of life." The Law on the Protection of Women's Rights and Interests provides for equality in ownership of property, inheritance rights, access to education, and equal pay for equal work. The ACWF was the leading implementer of women's policy for the government, and the State Council's National Working Committee on Children and Women coordinated women's policy. Many activists and observers expressed concern that discrimination was increasing. Women continued to report that discrimination, sexual harassment, unfair dismissal, demotion, and wage discrepancies were significant problems.

Authorities often did not enforce laws protecting the rights of women. According to legal experts, it was difficult to litigate sex-discrimination suits because of vague legal definitions. Some observers noted that the agencies tasked with protecting women's rights tended to focus on maternity-related benefits and wrongful termination during maternity leave rather than on sex discrimination, violence against women, and sexual harassment.

Despite government policies mandating nondiscrimination in employment and remuneration, women reportedly earned 66 percent as much as men. The Ministry of Human Resources and Social Security and the local labor bureaus are responsible for ensuring that enterprises complied with the labor law and the employment promotion law, each of which contains antidiscrimination provisions.

Many employers preferred to hire men to avoid the expense of maternity leave and childcare (paid paternity leave exists for men in some localities, but there is no national provision for paternity leave). Work units were allowed to impose an earlier mandatory retirement age for women than for men, and some employers lowered the effective retirement age for female workers to 50. In general the official retirement age for men was 60 and for women 55. Lower retirement ages also reduced pensions, which generally were based on the number of years worked. Job advertisements for women sometimes specified height and age requirements.

Women's rights advocates indicated that in rural areas women often forfeited land and property rights to their husbands in divorce proceedings. Rural contract law and laws protecting women's rights stipulate that women enjoy equal rights in cases of land management, but experts argued that this was rarely the case due to the complexity of the law and difficulties in its implementation. A 2011 interpretation of the country's marriage law by the Supreme People's Court exacerbated the gender wealth gap by stating that, after divorce, marital property belongs solely to the person registered as the homeowner in mortgage and registration documents – in most cases the husband. In determining child custody in divorce cases, judges make determinations based on the following guidelines: Children under age two should live with their mothers; custody of children two to nine years of age should be determined by who can provide the most stable living arrangement; and children 10 and over should be consulted when determining custody.

A high female suicide rate continued to be a serious problem. There were approximately 590 female suicides per day, according to a report released in September 2012 by the Chinese Center for Disease and Control and Prevention. This was more than the approximately 500 per day reported in 2009. The report noted that the suicide rate for women was three times higher than for men. Many observers believed that violence against women and girls, discrimination in education and employment, the traditional preference for male children, birth- limitation policies, and other societal factors contributed to the high female suicide rate. Women in rural areas, where the suicide rate for women was three to four times higher than for men, were especially vulnerable.

The World Bank reported that in 2009, 99 percent of women between the ages of 15 and 24 were literate, with a literacy rate of 91 percent for women above 15 compared with 97 percent for men above 15.

Women faced discrimination in higher education. The required score for the National Higher Entrance Exam was lower for men than for women at several universities. According to 2010 Ministry of Education statistics, women accounted for 49.6 percent of undergraduate students and 50.3 percent of master's students in 2012 but only 35 percent of doctoral students. Women with advanced degrees reported discrimination in the hiring process, since the job distribution system became more competitive and market driven.

Gender-based Sex Selection: According to the 2010 national census, the national average male-female sex ratio at birth was 118 to 100. Sex identification and sex- selective abortion were prohibited, but the practices continued because of traditional preference for male children and the birth-limitation policy.

Children

Birth Registration: Citizenship is derived from parents. Parents must register their children in compliance with the national household registration system within one month of birth. Unregistered children cannot access public services. No data was available on the number of unregistered births.

Education: Although the law provides for nine years of compulsory education for children, in economically disadvantaged rural areas many children did not attend school for the required period; some never attended. Although public schools were not allowed to charge tuition, faced with insufficient local and central government funding, many schools continued to charge miscellaneous fees. Such fees and other school-related expenses made it difficult for poorer families and some migrant workers to send their children to school.

In 2010 the official literacy rate for youth (defined as persons between the ages of 15 and 24) was 99 percent. The proportion of girls attending school in rural and minority areas was reportedly smaller than in cities. In rural areas 61 percent of boys and 43 percent of girls completed education at a grade higher than lower middle school. The government reported that nearly 20 million children of migrant laborers followed their parents to urban areas. Denied access to state-run schools, most children of migrant workers who attended school did so at unlicensed and poorly equipped schools.

Medical Care: Female babies suffered from a higher mortality rate than male babies, which was contrary to the worldwide norm. State media reported that infant mortality rates in rural areas were 27 percent higher for girls than boys and that neglect was one factor in their lower survival rate.

Child Abuse: The physical abuse of children can be grounds for criminal prosecution. Kidnapping, buying, and selling children for adoption increased during the past several years, particularly in poor rural areas. There were no reliable estimates of the number of children kidnapped, but according to media reports as many as 20,000 children were kidnapped every year for illegal adoption. Most children kidnapped internally were sold to couples unable to have children. Those convicted of buying an abducted child may be sentenced to three years' imprisonment. In the past most children rescued were boys, but increased demand for children reportedly drove traffickers to focus on girls as well. The Ministry of Public Security maintained a DNA database of parents of missing children and children recovered in law enforcement operations in an effort to reunite families.

Forced and Early Marriage: The legal minimum age for marriage is 22 for men and 20 for women. Child marriage was not known to be a problem, but there were reports of babies sold to be future brides. For example, families would adopt and raise babies for eventual marriage to their sons.

Sexual Exploitation of Children: By law those who force young girls under age 14 into prostitution may be sentenced to 10 years to life in prison, in addition to a fine or confiscation of property. If the case is especially serious, violators can receive a life sentence or be sentenced to death, in addition to confiscation of property. Those inducing girls under age 14 into prostitution can be sentenced to five years or more in prison in addition to a fine. Those who visit female prostitutes under age 14 are subject to five years or more in prison in addition to paying a fine.

According to the law the minimum age for consensual sex is 14.

Pornography of any kind, including child pornography, is illegal. Under the criminal code, those producing, reproducing, publishing, selling, or disseminating obscene materials with the purpose of making a profit may be sentenced up to three years in prison or put under criminal detention or surveillance in addition to paying a fine. Offenders in serious cases may receive prison sentences of three to 10 years in addition to paying a fine. In especially serious cases offenders are to be sentenced to 10 years or more in prison or given a life sentence in addition to a fine or confiscation of property. Persons found disseminating obscene books, magazines, films, audio or video products, pictures, or other kinds of obscene materials, if the case is serious, may be sentenced up to two years in prison or put under criminal detention or surveillance. Persons organizing the broadcast of obscene motion pictures or other audio or video products may be sentenced up to three years in prison or put under criminal detention or surveillance in addition to paying a fine. If the case is serious they are to be sentenced to three to 10 years in prison in addition to paying a fine.

Those broadcasting or showing obscene materials to minors less than age 18 are to be "severely punished."

Infanticide or Infanticide of Children with Disabilities: The Law on the Protection of Juveniles forbids infanticide, but there was evidence that the practice continued. According to the National Population and Family-planning Commission, a handful of doctors were charged with infanticide under this law. Female infanticide, sex- selective abortions, and the abandonment and neglect of baby girls remained problems due to the traditional preference for sons and the coercive birth-limitation policy.

Displaced Children: There were between 150,000 and one million urban street children, according to state-run media. This number was even higher if the children of migrant workers who spent the day on the streets were included. In 2010 the ACWF reported that the number of children in rural areas left behind by their migrant-worker parents totaled 58 million, 40 million under the age of 14.

Institutionalized Children: The law forbids the mistreatment or abandonment of children. The vast majority of children in orphanages were girls, many of whom were abandoned. Boys in orphanages were usually disabled or in poor health. Medical professionals sometimes advised parents of children with disabilities to put the children into orphanages.

The government denied that children in orphanages were mistreated or refused medical care but acknowledged that the system often was unable to provide adequately for some children, particularly those with serious medical problems. Adopted children were counted under the birth-limitation regulations in most locations. As a result, couples who adopted abandoned infant girls were sometimes barred from having additional children.

International Child Abductions: The country is not a party to the 1980 Hague Convention on the Civil Aspects of International Child Abduction. For information see the Department of State's report at travel.state.

Anti-Semitism

There were no reports of anti-Semitic acts during the year. The government does not recognize Judaism as an ethnicity or religion. According to information from the Jewish Virtual Library, the country's Jewish population was 2,500 in 2012.

Trafficking in Persons

See the Department of State's *Trafficking in Persons Report* at www.state.

Persons with Disabilities

The law protects the rights of persons with disabilities and prohibits discrimination, but conditions for such persons lagged far behind legal dictates and failed to provide persons with disabilities access to programs intended to assist them.

According to Article 3 of the Law on the Protection of Disabled Persons, "disabled persons are entitled to enjoyment of equal rights as other citizens in political, economic, cultural, and social fields, in family life and other aspects. The rights of disabled persons as citizens and their personal dignity are protected by law. Discrimination against, insult of, and infringement upon disabled persons is prohibited."

The Ministry of Civil Affairs and the China Disabled Persons Federation (CDPF), a government-organized civil association, are the main entities responsible for persons with disabilities. In June the CDPF stated that, based on 2010 census figures, 85 million persons with disabilities lived in the country. According to government statistics, in 2011 there were 5,254 vocational training facilities, which provided training for 299,000 persons with disabilities. Of the 32 million persons with disabilities of working age, more than 22 million were employed. Government statistics stated that 7.4 million persons with disabilities enjoyed "minimum-life-guarantee" stipends, and nearly three million had social insurance.

The law prohibits discrimination against minors with disabilities and codifies a variety of judicial protections for juveniles. In 2007 the Ministry of Education reported that nationwide there were 1,618 schools for children with disabilities. According to NGOs, there were approximately 20 million children with disabilities, only 2 percent of whom had access to education that could meet their needs.

According to the CDPF, in 2010 more than 519,000 school-age children with disabilities received compulsory education, 68 percent of them in inclusive education, and 32 percent in 1,705 special schools and 2,775 special classes. NGOs claimed that, while the overall school enrollment rate was 99 percent, only 75 percent of children with disabilities were enrolled in school. Nationwide, an estimated 243,000 school-age children with disabilities did not attend school. In 2011 a total of 7,150 persons with disabilities were admitted to standard colleges and universities.

Nearly 100,000 organizations existed, mostly in urban areas, to serve those with disabilities and protect their legal rights. The government, at times in conjunction with NGOs, sponsored programs to integrate persons with disabilities into society.

Misdiagnosis, inadequate medical care, stigmatization, and abandonment remained common problems. According to reports doctors frequently persuaded parents of children with disabilities to place their children in large government-run institutions where care was often inadequate. Those parents who chose to keep children with disabilities at home generally faced difficulty finding adequate medical care, day care, and education for their children. Government statistics showed that almost one-quarter of persons with disabilities lived in extreme poverty.

In part as a result of discrimination, unemployment among adults with disabilities remained a serious problem. The law requires local governments to offer incentives to enterprises that hire persons with disabilities. Regulations in some parts of the country also require employers to pay into a national fund for persons with disabilities when the employees with disabilities do not make up the statutory minimum percentage of the total workforce.

Standards adopted for making roads and buildings accessible to persons with disabilities are subject to the Law on the Handicapped, which calls for their "gradual" implementation. Compliance with the law was limited. The law permits universities to exclude candidates with disabilities who were otherwise qualified.

The law forbids the marriage of persons with certain mental disabilities, such as schizophrenia. If doctors find that a couple is at risk of transmitting congenital disabilities to their children, the couple may marry only if they agree to use birth control or undergo sterilization. The law stipulates that local governments must employ such practices to raise the percentage of births of children without disabilities.

National/Racial/Ethnic Minorities

Most minority groups resided in areas they traditionally inhabited. Government policy calls for members of recognized minorities to receive preferential treatment in birth planning, university admission, access to loans, and employment. Nonetheless, the substance and implementation of ethnic minority policies remained poor, and discrimination against minorities remained widespread.

Minority groups in border and other regions had less access to education than their Han counterparts, faced job discrimination in favor of Han migrants, and earned incomes well below those in other parts of the country. Government development programs often disrupted traditional living patterns of minority groups and included, in some cases, the forced relocation of persons. Han Chinese benefited disproportionately from government programs and economic growth. As part of its emphasis on building a "harmonious society" and maintaining social stability, the government downplayed racism and institutional discrimination against minorities, which remained the source of deep resentment in the XUAR, the Inner Mongolia Autonomous Region (IMAR), the TAR, and other Tibetan areas.

Ethnic minorities represented approximately 14 percent of delegates to the NPC and more than 15 percent of NPC Standing Committee members, according to an official report issued in 2011. A 2011 article in the official online news source for overseas readers stated that ethnic minorities comprised 41 percent of cadres in the Guangxi Zhuang Autonomous Region, 25 percent of cadres in Ningxia Hui Autonomous Region, and 51 percent of cadres in the XUAR. According to a July 2012 article from the official Xinhua News Agency, 32 percent of cadres in Yunnan Province were members of an ethnic minority. A June 5 government report stated that, of the 296 civil servants Guangxi Province recruited in 2012, almost 60 percent were ethnic minorities. During the year all five of the country's ethnic minority autonomous regions had chairmen (equivalent to the governor of a province) from minority groups. The CCP secretaries of these five autonomous regions were all Han. Han officials continued to hold the majority of the most powerful CCP and government positions in minority autonomous regions, particularly the XUAR.

The government's policy to encourage Han Chinese migration into minority areas significantly increased the population of Han in the XUAR. In recent decades the Han-Uighur ratio in the capital of Urumqi reversed from 20/80 to 80/20 and continued to be a source of Uighur resentment. Discriminatory hiring practices gave preference to Han and reduced job prospects for ethnic minorities. According to the 2010 national census, 8.75 million, or 40 percent, of the XUAR's 21.8 million official residents were Han. Hui, Kazakh, Kyrgyz, Uighur, and other ethnic minorities constituted approximately 13 million XUAR residents, or 60 percent of the total population. Official statistics understated the Han population, because they did not count the tens of thousands of Han Chinese who were long- term "temporary workers." As the government continued to promote Han migration into the XUAR and filled local jobs with domestic migrant labor, local officials coerced young Uighur women to participate in a government-sponsored labor transfer program to cities outside the XUAR, according to overseas human rights organizations.

The XUAR government took measures to dilute expressions of Uighur identity, including reducing the use of ethnic minority languages in XUAR schools and instituting Mandarin Chinese language requirements that disadvantaged ethnic- minority teachers. The government continued to apply policies that prioritized standard Chinese for instruction in school, thereby reducing or eliminating ethnic- language instruction. The dominant use of Mandarin Chinese in government, commerce, and academia disadvantaged graduates of minority-language schools who lacked Mandarin Chinese proficiency.

Authorities continued to implement repressive policies in the XUAR and targeted the region's ethnic Uighur population. Officials in the XUAR continued to implement a pledge to crack down on the government-designated "three forces" of religious extremism, "splittism," and terrorism, and they outlined efforts to launch a concentrated antiseparatist re-education campaign. Some raids, detentions, and judicial punishments ostensibly directed at individuals or organizations suspected of promoting the "three forces" appeared to be targeted at groups or individuals peacefully seeking to express their political or religious views. The government continued to repress Uighurs expressing peaceful political dissent and independent Muslim religious leaders, often citing counterterrorism as the reason for taking action.

According to the 2013 *China Law Yearbook*, authorities in 2012 arrested 1,105 individuals for "endangering state security," a 19 percent increase from 2011. The NGO Dui Hua estimated that arrests from Xinjiang accounted for 75 percent of "endangering state security" charges.

Uighurs continued to be sentenced to long prison terms, and in some cases executed without due process, on charges of separatism and endangering state security. The government pressured foreign countries to repatriate Uighurs, who faced the risk of imprisonment and mistreatment upon return. Some Uighurs refouled to China have simply disappeared.

Freedom of assembly was severely limited during the year in the XUAR. For information about violations of religious freedom in Xinjiang, please see the Department of State's *International Religious Freedom Report* at www.state.

Reportedly at year's end one son of exiled Uighur leader Rebiya Kadeer, president of the World Uighur Conference, whom the government blamed for orchestrating the 2009 riots in Urumqi, remained in prison.

Possession of publications or audiovisual materials discussing independence, autonomy, or other sensitive subjects was not permitted. Uighurs who remained in prison at year's end for their peaceful expression of ideas the government found objectionable included Abduhelil Zunun. Reportedly, Uighur poet Nurmuhemmet Yasin, originally imprisoned in 2005, died in prison in 2011.

XUAR and national-level officials defended the campaign against the three forces of religious extremism, "splittism," and terrorism and other policies as necessary to maintain public order. Officials continued to use the threat of violence as justification for extreme security measures directed at the local population, journalists, and visiting foreigners.

The law criminalizes discussion of separatism on the internet and prohibits use of the internet in any way that undermines national unity. It further bans inciting ethnic separatism or "harming social stability," and requires internet service providers and network operators to set up monitoring systems or to strengthen existing ones and report violations of the law.

Han control of the region's political and economic institutions also contributed to heightened tension. Although government policies continued to allot economic investment in and brought economic improvements to the XUAR, Han residents received a disproportionate share of the benefits. Job advertisements often made clear that Uighur applicants would not be considered.

Reuters News Agency reported that in November police used electric batons to prevent approximately 100 ethnic Mongols from attending the trial of six nomadic herders charged with sabotaging production and intentionally destroying property. Authorities arrested the six herders in June after a confrontation with employees of a state-owned forestry company. Protests against land seizures occurred throughout the year across the IMAR, resulting in detentions and police abuse, as the regional government sought to implement Beijing's policy of resettling China's nomadic population.

Societal Abuses, Discrimination, and Acts of Violence Based on Sexual Orientation and Gender Identity

No laws criminalize private consensual same-sex activities between adults. Due to societal discrimination and pressure to conform to family expectations, most gay, lesbian, bisexual, and transgender (LGBT) persons refrained from publicly discussing their sexual orientation. Individual activists and organizations working on LGBT problems continued to report discrimination and harassment from authorities, similar to other organizations that accept funding from overseas.

In June 2012 the Beijing LGBT center was notified by property management that its lease would be terminated early due to complaints that it was too noisy. Neighbors reportedly pressured management to terminate the lease after learning that it was an LGBT organization. The center was able to recoup only less than one-half of its investment of RMB 11,000 ($1,800) for the move.

In September organizers of the China Charity Fair in Shenzhen, Guangdong Province, told two gay rights advocacy groups that they could not display their advertisements and informational brochures because they were not registered with the Ministry of Civil Affairs. One of the advocacy groups attempting to participate reported that his organization unsuccessfully sought to register with the ministry for several years, despite making dozens of visits to local government offices.

In contrast with 2012, there reportedly was no government interference with the seventh Beijing Queer Film Festival. Organizers kept a low profile.

Other Societal Violence or Discrimination

The law prohibits discrimination against persons carrying infectious diseases and allows such persons to work as civil servants. The law does not address some common types of discrimination in employment, including discrimination based on height, physical appearance, or ethnic identity.

Despite provisions in the law, discrimination against persons with HIV/AIDS and hepatitis B carriers (including 20 million chronic carriers) remained widespread in many areas, and local governments sometimes tried to suppress their activities. In August 2012 a man who was refused employment after it was discovered he had hepatitis was awarded RMB 8,000 ($1,310) in damages by a Xi'an court.

HIV/AIDS activist Wan Yanhai, founder and director of the Beijing-based NGO Aizhixing, remained overseas after leaving the country in 2010. The organization continued to come under pressure from the government.

Western media reported that on May 30, Guangxi activist Ye Haiyan, who advocated for the rights of prostitutes and persons infected with HIV/AIDS, was beaten in her home by a group of 10 police officers before being detained at the local police station in Bobai County.

While in the past, persons with HIV/AIDS were routinely denied admission to hospitals, discrimination was less overt, and some hospitals came up with excuses for not being able to treat them. The hospitals feared that, should the general population find out that they were treating HIV/AIDS patients, patients would choose to go elsewhere. It was common practice for general hospitals to refer patients to specialty hospitals working with infectious diseases.

International involvement in HIV/AIDS prevention, care, and treatment, as well as central government pressure on local governments to respond appropriately, brought improvements in many localities. Some hospitals that previously refused to treat HIV/AIDS patients had active care and treatment programs because domestic and international training programs improved the understanding of local health-care workers and their managers. In Beijing dozens of local community centers encouraged and facilitated HIV/AIDS support groups.

In March 2012 Zhejiang Province eliminated its mandatory HIV testing for suspects arrested for drug charges, a move seen as a step in protecting the privacy of the individuals.

On July 1, Guangxi Zhuang Autonomous Region implemented new legislation requiring real name registration for HIV testing and obliging individuals who tested positive inform their spouses.

Despite a 2010 nationwide rule banning mandatory hepatitis B virus tests in job and school admissions applications, 61 percent of state-run companies in 2011 continued to use hepatitis B testing as a part of their preemployment screen.

A 2011 report from a Beijing-based NGO stated that 32 percent of kindergartens surveyed would refuse to enroll children infected with hepatitis B.

In July 2012 a widely used public health website for persons infected with hepatitis was blocked within the country. The website had been blocked two times earlier, in 2007 and 2008. The website's main goal is to eliminate discrimination of hepatitis carriers and provide a social forum to build awareness of the disease.

In October the Ministry of Commerce posted online for public consultation draft regulations that would ban individuals with AIDS from entering public bathhouses. The draft regulations stipulated a fine of RMB 30,000 ($4,910) for violators and mandated that all spas, hot springs, and bathhouses post anti-HIV/AIDS visitor signs on their premises. At year's end the draft regulations remained under review.

SECTION 7. WORKER RIGHTS

a. Freedom of Association and the Right to Collective Bargaining

The law does not provide for freedom of association, and workers are not free to organize or join unions of their own choosing. Independent unions are illegal, workers are not free to organize, and the right to strike is not protected in law.

The Trade Union Law gives the All-China Federation of Trade Unions (ACFTU) control over all union organizations and activities, including enterprise-level unions. The ACFTU is a CCP organ chaired by a member of the Politburo and is tasked to "uphold the leadership of the Communist Party." The ACFTU and its provincial and local branches continued aggressively to organize new constituent unions and add new members, especially in large, multinational enterprises.

According to the ACFTU the total trade union membership reached 280 million during the year, 109 million of whom were rural-urban migrant workers.

The law provides specific legal protections against antiunion discrimination and specifies that union representatives may not be transferred or terminated by enterprise management during their term of office. While there were no publicly available official statistics on the enforcement of these laws, there were periodic domestic media reports of courts awarding monetary compensation for wrongful terminations of union representatives.

The Trade Union Law specifically assigns the ACFTU and affiliated unions the responsibility to "coordinate the labor relations and safeguard the labor rights and interests of the enterprise employees through equal negotiation and collective contract system" and to represent employees in negotiating and signing collective contracts with enterprises or public institutions. The law states that trade union representatives at each level should be elected.

The Labor Dispute Mediation and Arbitration Law provides for labor dispute resolution through a three-stage process: mediation between the parties, arbitration by officially designated arbitrators, and litigation. A key article of this law requires employers to consult with labor unions or employee representatives on matters that have a direct bearing on the immediate interests of their workers.

The Labor Contract Law provides that labor unions "shall assist and direct the employees" in establishing "a collective negotiation mechanism" and that collective contracts can include "matters of remuneration, working hours, breaks, vacations, work safety and hygiene, insurance, benefits, etc." It further provides that there may be industrial or regional collective contracts "in industries such as construction, mining, catering services, etc. in the regions at or below the county level."

The labor law allows for collective bargaining for workers in all types of enterprises, and collective contract regulations provide protections against discrimination and unfair dismissal for employee representatives during collective consultations. Regulations require a union to gather input from workers prior to consultation with management and to submit collective contracts to workers or their congress for approval. There is no legal obligation for employers to negotiate, and some employers refused to do so.

If collective bargaining negotiations do begin, there is no requirement for employers to bargain in good faith. If no agreement is reached, the employer does not have a right to lock out the workers, and the workers do not have a right to strike. While work stoppages are not expressly prohibited in law and it is not illegal for workers to strike spontaneously, Article 53 of the constitution has been interpreted as a ban on labor strikes by obligating all citizens to "observe labor discipline and public order."

Although the ACFTU, especially at provincial levels, often played an important role in advocacy for improved labor protections during 2012, this activism stalled during the year, in part due to a lack of clear direction from the Xi Jinping and Li Keqiang administration. During the ACFTU's 16th National Congress in October, high-level officials called on participants to improve the lives of workers through proactive employment policies, a better social safety net, and attention to safety in the workplace. They noted the need for both increased government enforcement and supervision and responsibility by trade unions and the public.

In November the CCP concluded a high-level meeting by issuing a resolution that outlined reforms with the potential to affect freedom of association and collective bargaining, including expanding the use of employees' representative committees and innovating channels for workers to make appeals. The role of the ACFTU in a strike is primarily limited to involvement in investigations and assistance to the Ministry of Human Resources and Social Security in resolving disputes.

ACFTU constituent unions were generally ineffective in representing and protecting the rights and interests of workers. This was particularly true in the case of migrant workers, who generally have less interaction with the ACFTU, who tend to work in foreign-invested enterprises, and for whom, especially among second-generation migrant workers, expectations of working conditions have increased. The ACFTU and the CCP maintain a variety of mechanisms to influence the selection of trade union representatives. Although the law states that trade union officers at each level should be elected, most factory-level officers were appointed by ACFTU-affiliated unions, often in coordination with employers, and were drawn largely from the ranks of management. Direct election by workers of union leaders continued to be rare, occurred only at the enterprise level, and was subject to supervision by higher levels of the union or the CCP. In enterprises where direct election of union officers took place, regional ACFTU officers and local CCP authorities retained control over the selection and approval of candidates. Even in these cases, workers and NGOs expressed concern about the sustainability of elections and the knowledge and capacity of elected union officials who often lacked collective bargaining skills.

In March 2012 the Fair Labor Association (FLA) and Apple drafted an action plan for remediation at Foxconn supplier facilities. A key component of this action plan was the establishment of union elections. In its final report the FLA verified that no workplace elections had been conducted in the three facilities (Guanlan, Longhua, and Chengdu) since the beginning of the year.

In a joint open letter to the Shenzhen Federation of Trade Unions (SFTU) in October, a group of students from nine universities in China outlined their findings in five Shenzhen factories at which the SFTU had purportedly adopted direct elections. While the elections did occur in many cases, the students found that trade union committees were still composed of members of company management. They also found that the union continued to fail to protect workers from basic labor law violations.

Many autonomous regions and municipalities enacted local rules allowing collective wage negotiation, and some limited form of collective bargaining was more or less compulsory in 25 of 31 provinces, according to the ACFTU. The Guangdong provincial government guidelines on enterprise collective wage bargaining require employers to give employee representatives information regarding a company's operations, including employee pay and benefits, to be used in wage bargaining. The guidelines also allow the local labor bureau, if requested by the employees and employers, to act as a mediator to help determine wage increases.

Despite the Labor Contract Law's provisions for collective consultation related to common areas of dispute such as wages, hours, days off, and benefits, noncompliance with this provision, even at the minimum levels required by law, was common. Instead, tactics used by management included forcing employees to sign blank contracts and failing to provide workers a copy of their contract. Lack of government resources also undermined effective implementation and enforcement of the Labor Contract Law.

The number of labor disputes nationwide continued to rise as workers' awareness of the laws increased. According to figures from the Ministry of Human Resources and Social Security, as of September 2012, there were more than 3,000 labor arbitration units and 25,000 labor arbitrators. Through 2011 the Ministry of Human Resources and Social Security handled 1.3 million "labor and personnel disputes." Of these, 589,000 were registered arbitration cases, of which 93.9 percent were resolved. Most formal dispute resolution continued to occur between individual workers and employers, rather than managing collective disputes. The relevant regulations and rules address predominantly rights-based, rather than interest-based, disputes.

Strikes primarily continued to be resolved directly between workers and management without the involvement of the ACFTU or its constituent local trade unions. In order to avoid strikes or address minor labor relations disputes, factory management continued to prefer to engage directly with workers via labor- management committees, rather than through the legally approved ACFTU- affiliated trade union. The Ministry of Human Resources and Social Security voiced support for the expansion and establishment of labor-management committees throughout all enterprises. Labor NGOs often provided information, training, and legal support to workers on collective bargaining and dispute resolution, in lieu of effective support by the ACFTU.

There continued to be reports of workers throughout the country engaging in strikes, work stoppages, and other protest actions. Although the government restricted the release of figures for the number of strikes and protests each year, the frequency of "spontaneous" strikes remained high, especially in Shenzhen and other areas with developed labor markets and large pools of sophisticated, rights- conscious workers. Local government responses to strikes varied, with some jurisdictions showing tolerance for strikes while others continued to treat worker protests as illegal demonstrations.

In January, Hong Kong media reported that thousands of workers from the Panzhihua Iron and Steel Group in Chengdu took to the streets to demand wage increases. Authorities deployed 1,000 police to suppress the march and to disperse the crowd after a confrontation with the protesters. Chinese-language media reported that on November 7, police dispersed 200 striking workers at a Dongguan toy factory, and that authorities beat and arrested numerous workers.

Workers engaged in collective action for a number of reasons. In many cases striking workers called attention to wage arrears, insufficient pay, and poor working conditions. New areas of disputes included factory closure or relocation, severance pay and other compensation, and benefits such as pensions. Although a large number of the major strikes reported in the media occurred in the Pearl River Delta, labor unrest was widespread throughout the country. Small-scale worker protests and strikes regularly occurred in Shanghai and Zhejiang, Jiangsu, and Anhui provinces.

Workers increasingly went on strike to demand payment of past wages, as an economic downturn led to diminishing profits, more factory closures, and abandoned construction projects. On March 6, nearly 1,000 workers at an electronics factory in Dongguan, Guangdong Province, protested and blocked roads over compensation problems.

Strikes also occurred in an increasingly broad range of sectors. While many strikes occurred in manufacturing, reports increased of strikes in the transport, sanitation, and service industries similarly stemming from failure to gain adequate compensation. In August a hospital in Guangzhou attempted to impose a management-dictated settlement for unpaid overtime on a group of hospital security guards. Despite threats of dismissal, the guards went on strike. Management refused to negotiate with the guards, and local authorities detained them for staging an illegal demonstration.

In August an estimated 3,000 workers at a toy factory in Shenzhen conducted a solidarity strike in support of 551 long-term migrant workers also at the factory. Despite having employed the workers for well over the 15 years required for pension eligibility, the company had failed to make mandatory contributions to their pension funds prior to 2008. Facing retirement, these workers were not able to claim the pensions to which they were entitled.

In May informally elected workers' representatives at Shenzhen Diweixin furniture factory led a protest against their employers over the company's refusal to discuss compensation for a planned relocation. On May 23, authorities detained worker leader Wu Guijun after protracted strikes and petitions to the city government to intervene in fruitless negotiations. According to independent labor organizations, Wu was formally charged with "assembling a crowd to disturb social order" on September 28, but later reports indicated that the procuratorate refused to accept the charges due to lack of evidence and sent the case back to the public security officials for further investigation. Wu remained in detention as of year's end.

Other labor activists detained in previous years reportedly remained in detention at year's end, including Chen Yong, Kong Youping, Liu Jian, Liu

Jianjun, Memet Turghun Abdulla, Wang Miaogen, Xing Shiku, Zhou Decai, Zhu Chengzhi, and Zhu Fangming.

b. Prohibition of Forced or Compulsory Labor

The law prohibits forced and compulsory labor, but there were reports that forced labor of adults and children occurred (see section 7.c.).

There were reports that employers withheld wages or required unskilled workers to deposit several months' wages as security against the workers departing early from their labor contracts. These practices often prevented workers from exercising their right to leave their employment and made them vulnerable to forced labor. Implementation of amended labor laws, along with workers' increased knowledge of their rights under these new laws, continued to reduce these practices.

International NGOs alleged that provincial and local governments were complicit in some cases of forced labor of university students as "interns" at facilities managed by the Taiwanese electronics giant Foxconn. Local governments, in order to encourage Foxconn to establish operations in their cities, promised to help recruit workers for Foxconn's labor-intensive operations. In September the media reported that students in Shandong and Jiangsu provinces complained that their universities made it mandatory that they serve 45-day internships on assembly lines in Foxconn factories to meet Foxconn's production demands. A December 12 FLA report of Foxconn facilities in Guanlan, Longhua, and Chengdu indicated that no student interns had been employed at those sites during the year.

Forced labor in penal institutions remained a serious problem, according to the International Trade Union Confederation. Many prisoners and detainees were required to work, often with no remuneration. Compulsory labor of detainees in RTL facilities, who had not been tried and convicted in a competent court, also constituted forced labor.

In both cases detainees reportedly experienced harsh and exploitative conditions of work, including long periods without a rest day and often working more than 10, and sometimes 12 or 14, hours per day to meet informal "quotas" imposed by facility management. Detainees who did not meet their quota were threatened with physical violence and other forms of punishment.

In addition there were credible allegations that prisoners were forced to work for private production facilities associated with prisons. These facilities often operated under two different names, a prison name and a commercial enterprise name. No effective mechanism prevented the export of goods made under such conditions.

Goods and materials likely to be produced by forced labor included toys, garments and textiles, electronics, bricks, and coal.

The Ministry of Justice discussed allegations of exported prison-labor goods with foreign government officials, but information about prisons, including associated labor camps and factories, was tightly controlled. Although the ministry has official control over the RTL system, police and other local authorities had a great degree of influence on a case-by-case basis.

In November 2012 a Chongqing court rejected the wrongful imprisonment suit brought by Ren Jianyu, who had been released from an RTL center one year into his two-year sentence for "incitement to subvert state power" for posting online statements critical of the political system. In July, Ren submitted an application to the Chongqing RTL committee requesting compensation totaling RMB 167,762 ($27,440) to cover the wages he lost while in the camp and the psychological harm he suffered.

After the Standing Committee of the NPC voted to abolish the RTL system in December (see section 1.d.), media and NGO reports indicated that many of the RTL facilities were converted to drug rehabilitation centers or prisons. It is not clear whether forced labor continued in these facilities.

Also see the Department of State's Trafficking in Persons Report at www.state.

c. Prohibition of Child Labor and Minimum Age for Employment

The law prohibits the employment of children under the age of 16. It refers to workers between the ages of 16 and 18 as "juvenile workers" and prohibits them from engaging in certain forms of dangerous work, including in mines.

The law specifies administrative review, fines, and revocation of business licenses of those businesses that illegally hired minors and provides that underage children found working should be returned to their parents or other custodians in their original place of residence. The penalty for employing children under 16 in hazardous labor or for excessively long hours ranges from three to seven years' imprisonment, but a significant gap remained between legislation and implementation.

Child labor remained a problem. Print media and online reports most frequently documented the use of child labor in the electronics manufacturing industry, although many reports indicated it occurred in a number of sectors.

The government does not publish statistics on the extent of child labor, but rising wages and a tightening labor market led some companies to seek to hire underage workers in violation of the law. Some local authorities also ignored the practice of child labor or even facilitated it to prevent employers from moving to other areas.

Reports of child labor persisted in areas suffering from labor shortages and in smaller enterprises that compensated workers on a piece-rate basis. For example, in Dongguan, Guangdong Province, a manufacturing hub hit hard by labor shortages and rising wages, local employers admitted that the use of child labor on a temporary basis was common. Although Dongguan Bureau of Human Resources and Social Security statistics showed an increase in child labor cases, the bureau did not have sufficient resources to increase enforcement operations among the thousands of small enterprises operating in the area.

In May a 14-year-old boy working at an electronics factory in Dongguan died suddenly in the factory dormitory. The boy used a false identity card to gain employment, and local officials cited the company for violating child labor laws.

In an open letter to the Guangdong Province Communist Party secretary posted on the internet, the mother of a 15-year-old boy from Henan, burned badly in 2012 while working in a Zhuhai electronics factory, appealed for help in obtaining compensation for the injury. The employer had refused to pay both the compensation sought by the family and the award subsequently determined by the labor arbitration board. Provincial authorities fined the employer and urged the local labor bureau to expedite the case, but compensation for the injury was still pending at year's end.

On December 27, the Guangzhou-based *Southern Metropolis Daily* reported that approximately 70 underage workers were discovered working at an electronics company in Shenzhen's Baoan District. The alleged underage workers were all from the Yi ethnic minority group, and all were from a remote mountainous region of Liangshan, Sichuan Province, the origin of several recent child-labor trafficking cases. This followed incidents in 2011 and 2008 involving underage workers from the same region. Although in each instance local labor authorities intervened after the *Southern Metropolis Daily* notified them of the underage workers, the three similar cases reflect a systemic inability to deter trafficking of underage workers or to identify child labor through regular labor inspections. In the most recent case the Shenzhen company posted a notice on its website blaming the company's labor dispatch service provider for providing worker identity cards purporting to show all of them to be older than age 16.

Abuse of the student-worker system continued as well. One international labor NGO reported that most students working in domestic companies in the supply chains of multinational electronics manufacturers, where there was greater scrutiny, did not have the formal written contracts required by law. After an internal audit, one multinational electronics company admitted it had violated the labor law after interns between the ages of 14 and 16 were discovered working at its subsidiary in Yantai, Shandong Province.

As in past years, there continued to be allegations that schools and local officials improperly facilitated the supply of student laborers. Some reports indicated that schools supplied factories with illegal child labor under the pretext of vocational training, in some cases making this labor compulsory for the student.

d. Acceptable Conditions of Work

There was no national minimum wage, but the law requires local and provincial governments to set their own minimum wage according to standards promulgated by the Ministry of Human Resources and Social Security. Average wage levels continued to increase. Monthly minimum wages varied greatly with Shenzhen, Guangdong Province, reaching RMB 1,600 ($262) from March 1 and towns in remote Ningxia Province the lowest at RMB 750 ($123). During the year the country increased its "rural poverty level" to RMB 192 ($31.40) per month.

The law mandates a 40-hour standard workweek, excluding overtime, and a 24- hour weekly rest period. It also prohibits overtime work in excess of three hours per day or 36 hours per month and mandates premium pay for overtime work.

A regulation states that labor and social security bureaus at or above the county level are responsible for enforcement of labor law. The law also provides that where the ACFTU finds an employer in violation of the regulation, it shall have the power to demand that the relevant local labor bureaus deal with the case.

Many vulnerable workers, including those older workers laid off as a result of restructuring of state-owned enterprise, as well as many rural-urban migrants, were employed in the informal economy. In 2012 Chinese Academy of Social Sciences' researchers estimated that the prevalence of informal employment ranged from 20 to 37 percent overall, based on the definition used, with between 45 and 65 percent of migrants employed in the informal sector. UN experts reported that women were particularly active in the informal economy, often as domestic workers or petty entrepreneurs. Micro- and small businesses with fewer than seven employees also meet the international criteria for informality. Workers in the informal sector often lacked coverage under labor contracts, and even with contracts migrant workers in particular had less access to benefits, especially social insurance. Workers in the informal sector worked longer hours and earned one-half to two- thirds as much as comparable workers in the formal sector.

The State Administration for Work Safety (SAWS) sets and enforces occupational health and safety regulations. The Law on Prevention and Control of Occupational Diseases requires employers to provide free health checkups for employees working in hazardous conditions and to inform them of the results. Companies that violate the regulation have their operations suspended or are deprived of business certificates and licenses.

Effective May 2012 the SAWS and the Ministry of Finance jointly issued the *Measures on Incentives for Safe Production Reporting*, which authorize cash rewards to whistleblowers reporting companies for violations, such as concealing workplace accidents, operating without proper licensing, operating unsafe equipment, or failing to provide workers with adequate safety training. The measures warn against false accusations but also stipulate protection under the law for legitimate whistleblowers who report violations.

While many labor laws and regulations on worker safety were fully compatible with international standards, implementation and enforcement were generally poor due to a lack of adequate resources. Compliance with the law was weak, and standards were regularly violated. While excessive overtime occurred, in many cases workers encouraged noncompliance by requesting greater amounts of overtime to counterbalance low base wages and increase their overall wages. Inadequately enforced labor laws, occupational health and safety laws, and regulations continued to put workers' livelihoods, health, and safety at risk.

Almost all local and provincial governments raised minimum wage levels significantly during the year as a result of changing economic and demographic conditions. As the average tenure of workers in the Pearl River Delta increased, their skills improved, adding more upward pressure on wages. Spot shortages of skilled labor, increased inland investment, and successful strikes led to generally increased wage levels for workers in all parts of the country.

Nonpayment of wages remained a problem in many areas. Governments at various levels continued efforts to prevent arrears and to recover payment of unpaid wages and insurance contributions. It remained possible for companies to relocate or close on short notice, often leaving employees without adequate recourse for due compensation. In some extreme cases, workers who feared that they would be deprived of adequate compensation or severance engaged in actions such as taking managers hostage.

Although creative strategies by some multinational purchasers provided new approaches to reducing the incidence of labor violations in supplier factories, insufficient government oversight of both foreign affiliated and purely domestic supplier factories continued to contribute to poor working conditions. Questions related to acceptable working conditions, especially overtime, continued to plague electronics manufacturers such as Foxconn.

On December 12, the FLA released the third and final verification report on conditions at Foxconn facilities in China, tracking progress on that action plan through July 1. The report documented that nearly 100 percent of all actions recommended by the FLA had been completed at three key facilities in Guanlan, Longhua, and Chengdu, resulting in clear changes in company policy. Nonetheless, FLA assessors documented numerous violations of domestic law. While some workers received an average of one day off per week, others went for a month or more without these breaks. In some cases workers worked more than 60 hours per week, and for a six-month period, more than one-half of the workers in the Longhua and Guanlan facilities exceeded the legal overtime limit of 36 hours per month. In Chengdu from July to October more than 75 percent of workers exceeded this limit.

Although SAWS reported that the rate of industrial accidents continued to decline, there were several high-profile instances of industrial accidents. On June 3, a total of 121 workers died in a fire that swept through a poultry-processing plant in the northeastern province of Jilin. In that incident most of the exits at the plant had been locked from outside, and none of the 395 employees working at the time had received fire safety training. SAWS responded by dispatching teams to assess safety standards at factories. Although inspections routinely identified existing problems that increased the risk of industrial accidents, ensuring that companies acted on the findings of the inspections remained a challenge.

Authorities continued to press mines to improve safety measures and mandated greater investments in safety. In August 2012 SAWS announced its goal of closing hundreds of small coalmines during the year in an attempt to reduce the number of deadly accidents.

Despite consistent reductions in mining deaths, there continued to be many coalmine accidents throughout the country.

In Jilin Province, gas explosions at coalmines on March 29 and April 1 killed 53 workers. An third explosion on April 21, also in Jilin, killed 18 workers – despite an order for all coal mines in the province to suspend operations and undergo safety inspections following the earlier two explosions.

ACFTU occupational disease experts estimated that 200 million workers worked in hazardous environments. According to the Chinese Center for Disease Control and Prevention, only an estimated 10 percent of eligible employees received regular occupational health services. Small- and medium-sized enterprises, the largest employers, often failed to provide the required health services. They also did not provide proper safety equipment that could help prevent disease, and were rarely required to pay compensation to victims and their families. Instances of pneumoconiosis, or black lung disease, remained high. A charitable NGO that helped to treat migrant workers estimated the disease affected approximately six million rural residents.

In: Human Rights in China   ISBN: 978-1-63463-180-8
Editor: Kimberly Austin   © 2014 Nova Science Publishers, Inc.

Chapter 3

PRISON LABOR EXPORTS FROM CHINA AND IMPLICATIONS FOR U.S. POLICY[*]

John Dotson and Teresa Vanfleet

Disclaimer: This paper is the product of professional research performed by staff of the U.S.-China Economic and Security Review Commission, and was prepared at the request of the Commission to support its deliberations. Posting of the report to the Commission's website is intended to promote greater public understanding of the issues addressed by the Commission in its ongoing assessment of U.S.-China economic relations and their implications for U.S. security, as mandated by Public Law 106-398 and Public Law 108-7. However, the public release of this document does not necessarily imply an endorsement by the Commission, any individual Commissioner, or the Commission's professional staff, of the views or conclusions expressed in this staff research report.

EXECUTIVE SUMMARY

Since the Commission's examination in 2008 of prison labor issues in the People's Republic of China (PRC), there has been little substantive reduction in the scale and scope of China's broad network of prison labor facilities. These facilities, led by local officials, continue to produce goods intended for

---

[*] This is an edited, reformatted and augmented version of a Staff Research Report released by the U.S.-China Economic and Security Review Commission, July 9, 2014.

export, including online goods and services,[1] on a potentially large scale, in violation of U.S.-China agreements on the exports of prison labor goods to the United States. Further, it is unclear whether the recent abolition of "reeducation through labor" (RTL)[2] and reported release of up to tens of thousands of prisoners will have a significant impact on the prison labor system and export of prison labor products.

Although U.S. representatives in Beijing have continued to engage with their Chinese counterparts regarding suspected prison manufacturing facilities, the pattern of long delays and minimal cooperation by officials in the PRC Ministry of Prisons persists. Allegations of prison labor exports from China to the United States and other countries continue to surface, raising legitimate doubts regarding the effectiveness of current enforcement mechanisms.

The Commission's Definition of "Prison Labor"

The Chinese government in general adopts the position that RTL facilities (as well as other institutions for non-judicially imposed confinement) are distinct from "prisons." [1] In its *2008 Annual Report to Congress*, the Commission rejected this position:

The Commission believes that issues related to "prison labor" must be considered within the broader context of government-administered facilities in China in which detainees perform forced labor under penal conditions, regardless of whether such facilities are officially designated as "prisons" by the Chinese government. Therefore, the Commission has adopted this broader interpretation of forced labor under penal conditions as equating to "prison labor" for its consideration of issues related to alleged prison labor imports into the United States.

The Commission's interpretation is supported by existing U.S. law and legal precedent.[3]

---

[1] Such goods and services reportedly include the video game market where "gold farming" results in the potential sale or purchase of characters or commodities that Chinese prisoners have been forced to play and accrue increased value within the game. See more information on p. 8 of this report.

[2] The "reeducation through labor" program is an extrajudicial mechanism whereby local authorities may detain citizens for several years without trial. Xinhua (English edition), "China to Abolish Reeducation Through Labor," November 15, 2013. *http://news.xinhuanet.com/english/china/2013-11/15/c_132891921.htm.*

[3] Text from the Tariff Act of 1930 emphasizes that *forced labor* is central to the law's intent: "'Forced labor,' as herein used, shall mean all work or service which is exacted from any person under the menace of any penalty for its nonperformance and for which the worker

Using the Commission's 2008 definition of prison labor, this staff report considers all forced labor detention facilities in China – to include RTL sites – to be prison labor facilities. [2]

THE SCOPE AND ROLE OF CHINA'S PRISON LABOR SYSTEM

China's network of penal forced labor facilities,[4] established in the early years of the Chinese Communist Party (CCP) government to hold both criminals and political dissidents, remains in operation today. [3] Over time, the system has served many roles, including as a means for criminal punishment and rehabilitation, economic production, and political repression. [4]

A complete and rigorous analysis of the scope and role of China's prison labor system is difficult to conduct because the Chinese government classifies most information related to the prison system as a state secret, including its size and details of its operations. [5] Additionally, available anecdotal information is fragmented or poorly corroborated. In at least one known instance, Beijing arrested a naturalized U.S. citizen raised in China and charged him with espionage for gathering information on prison labor camps.[5] Analysis is further complicated by the distinction generally drawn by the Chinese government between "prison" facilities and RTL facilities (see Table 1), and it is unclear the extent to which forced labor is incorporated into China's prison system at large.

---

does not offer himself voluntarily." Tariff Act of 1930, 19 U.S. Code 19 § 1307, "Convict-Made Goods; Importation Prohibited." *http://www.law.cornell.edu/uscode/text/19/1307*. In 1994, the U.S. Court of International Trade ruled that China's reeducation through labor facilities were "forced labor institutions," and that goods produced by such facilities were subject to the provisions of 19 U.S. Code 19 § 1307. U.S. Court of International Trade, ruling in the case of China Diesel Imports, Inc. v. United States (court no. 92-10 00696), December 7, 1994. *http://www.leagle.com/decision/19941217870FSupp347_11143.*

[4] This penal system of forced labor is also known as the "laogai" system.

[5] In June 1995, Hongda "Harry" Wu, a naturalized U.S. citizen, was arrested by PRC authorities in the vicinity of Wuhan (Hubei Province) for secretly gathering photos, film, and other documentation of prison camp facilities. He was later released with the assistance of U.S. diplomatic personnel. Seth Faison, "China Keeps Up Criticism as U.S. Welcomes Dissident," New York Times, August 26, 1995. http://www.nytimes.com/1995/08/26/world /china-keepsup-criticism-as-us-welcomes-dissident.html.

Table 1. Categories of Detention in the People's Republic of China

Criminal Sentences *(imposed by a court)*	Administrative Detentions *(imposed by police officials, with no legal due process required)*	Extralegal Forms of Detention *(no basis under PRC law)*
"Reform Through Labor" A formal sentence to confinement in a prison farm or factory. The Chinese government officially dropped this term, but it remains in widespread usage, and the practice continues. [6]	**"Reeducation Through Labor" (RTL)** A system of sentencing for up to three years (with possible extension for a fourth year) officially intended as a means to rehabilitate petty criminal offenders (e.g., thieves, drug abusers, sex workers). However, it has also been employed against political dissidents and petitioners seeking redress for grievances.[7] **"Forced Job Placement"** A system in which inmates who have completed their sentences may be forced to reside and work in or near their place of confinement, with continued restrictions on their personal liberty. [8] **"Custody and Education"** A sanction by which sex workers and their clients may be imprisoned for up to two years. [9] **"Custody and Rehabilitation"** A sanction by which juvenile offenders (under the age of 16) may be imprisoned for up to three years. [10]	**"Double Regulation"** A system by which Communist Party officials (often, but not necessarily, under investigation for corruption) may be confined incommunicado in secret locations for interrogation. [11] **"Soft Detention"** The practice of imposing de facto house arrest on dissidents, rights activists, and others who threaten "social stability." [12] **"Black Jails"** An unofficial system of unlicensed confinement facilities used by local officials primarily to detain petitioners seeking redress of grievances. [13] **"Psychiatric Confinement"** The practice by many local officials of ordering petitioners and others who "disturb social order" to be confined in mental hospitals. [14]

Working from the limited information available, analysts produce a broad range of assessments regarding the system's total size. For example, a 2013 report published by the U.S. Department of State (DoS) estimates China has 681 prisons, holding 1.64 million inmates, [15] while the non-profit Laogai Research Foundation identifies approximately 1,400 forced labor facilities of all types in China, [16] with an estimated prisoner population of over 3 million persons (see Figure 1). [17] Referring specifically to RTL detention sites, the official website of the Bureau of Reeducation Through Labor Administration under the Ministry of Justice published a rare article in 2011 stating that, as of late 2008, China held 160,000 prisoners in 350 RTL facilities nationwide. [18] However, other sources estimate the total number of RTL prisoners in 2013 to be 260,000. [19] Although precise data is unavailable, it is clear China's prison labor system is massive in scale.

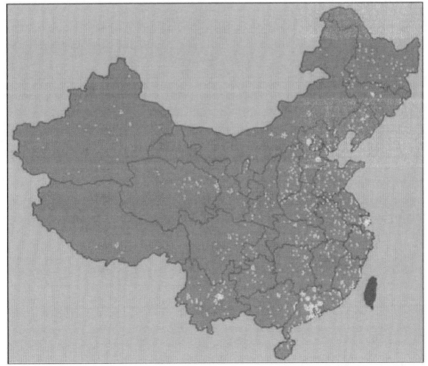

Source: Laogai Research Foundation, "What Is The Laogai System?"
http://www.laogai.org/page/what-laogai-system.

Figure 1. Forced Labor Detention Facilities in the People's Republic of China.

The Economic Role of the Prison Labor System

Since its inception, Chinese officials have viewed the prison labor system as an important source of economic production. In the 1980s, then paramount leader Deng Xiaoping emphasized the economic role of China's prison labor facilities, encouraging them to develop commercial enterprises – including export-oriented enterprises – to be financially self-supporting. [20] Because prisons serve a dual role as both correctional facilities and economic production centers, nearly every forced labor facility in China operates under the dual identity of its prison name as well as its commercial name. [21] For example, the "Yunnan No. 1 Prison" is also known as "Jinma Diesel Engine Plant."[6] Under the latter identity, such companies were once designated by the government as "special state-run enterprises." [22][7] Profitable prison companies help to fund the operations of both local and national government. Prison labor enterprises producing high-tech goods such as semiconductors and optical instruments are the most profitable, each earning an estimated annual revenue of tens of millions of USD and paying hundreds of thousands of USD annually in taxes to the Chinese government. [23]

Unpaid labor has historically underpinned the profitability of China's prisons. According to the 2012 *Trafficking in Persons Report* from DoS, "[t]he [PRC] government reportedly profits from [the use of] forced labor. Many prisoners and detainees in 'reeducation through labor' facilities [are] required to work, often with no remuneration." In addition to operating spinoff commercial enterprises, many prisons function as subcontractors for Chinese firms. DoS has noted cases in which "detainees were forced to work up to 18 hours a day without pay for private companies working in partnership with Chinese authorities" and "were beaten for failing to complete work quotas." [24]

---

[6] In 1991, the U.S. Commissioner of Customs issued a detention order for diesel engines manufactured by the "Golden Horse (Jinma) Diesel Factory" (Yunnan No. 1 Prison), on the grounds that their importation violated Section 307 of the Tariff Act of 1930. U.S. Customs and Border Protection, Convict, Forced, or Indentured Labor Product Importations. http://www.cbp.gov/trade.

[7] The Chinese government formerly identified prison production facilities as "special state-run enterprises" in published reference materials but ceased this practice in 1990 – likely as a result of foreign criticisms of its forced labor system. U.S. General Accounting Office, "Implementation of the 1992 Prison Labor Memorandum of Understanding," April 1995, p. 10. http://archive.gao.gov/t2pbat1/153806.pdf.

"Reeducation Through Labor" As a Tool of Political Repression

Most prisoners held in China's prison labor facilities are detained for non-political criminal offenses, though a significant minority are political prisoners in prisons, RTL facilities, as well as "black jails," mental institutions, and other forms of arbitrary detention. According to some estimates, China detains between 5,000 and 26,000 prisoners annually for political reasons. [25]

In particular, Chinese authorities have employed RTL as an extrajudicial tool to suppress ethnic and religious groups it views as subversive. According to one former prisoner, the Masanjia RTL facility, discussed later in this report, holds approximately 470 prisoners divided into three brigades, with one brigade reserved for members of Falun Gong, a spiritual movement banned in China. Accounts from other prisoners indicate approximately half the inmates held at Masanjia[8] were members of either Falun Gong or unregistered Christian churches. [26] Sentencing to RTL has also has been levied against Uighurs and Tibetans for allegedly petitioning the government or leading protests. [27] According to the DoS's 2013 *Trafficking in Persons Report*, Chinese prison labor facilities continue to hold many political prisoners, including rights activists, relatives of Uighur activists, labor activists, a Roman Catholic bishop, and a Tibetan Buddhist monk. [28]

PRC COMPLIANCE WITH U.S.-CHINA PRISON LABOR EXPORT AGREEMENTS

U.S. law prohibits the importation of goods produced "wholly or in part in any foreign country by convict labor or/and forced labor or/and indentured labor under penal sanctions."[9] As U.S. trade with China expanded dramatically in the 1980s and 1990s, so did concern in Congress regarding the importation into the United States of goods purportedly produced through prison labor in China.[10] This concern was raised in debates surrounding China's entry into the

---

[8] See more information on the Masanjia case on p. 9 of this report.

[9] The law in question is the Tariff Act of 1930, 19 U.S. Code 19 § 1307, "Convict-Made Goods; Importation Prohibited." See Appendix 1 of this report for further discussion on U.S. law pertaining to the importation of prison labor products.

[10] For example, in November 1991 a concurrent resolution of the U.S. Congress stated that "[w]hereas forced labor is an integral part of the Chinese prison system, and Chinese prisoners are forced to labor under extremely inhumane and dangerous conditions with little or no compensation for their work; Whereas ... Chinese prisons seek to export forced labor products to the United States, and have devised numerous methods to evade United States

World Trade Organization (WTO) as well as the granting of permanent most-favored nation (MFN) trading status to China.[11]

To address Congressional concerns and smooth the way for China's ascension to the WTO, the U.S. and China produced two bilateral diplomatic agreements: a 1992 "Memorandum of Understanding" (MOU) that laid out general principles for stopping bilateral trade in prison labor goods; and a 1994 "Statement of Cooperation" (SOC) that established more specific procedures for site inspections at prison labor facilities suspected of producing goods for export.[12]

As part of its legislative mandate, the U.S.-China Economic and Security Review Commission is tasked by Congress to assess and report on "the degree of non-compliance by the People's Republic of China with agreements... on prison labor imports... and United States enforcement policies with respect to such agreements."[29][13] The Commission's detailed examination of this matter in 2008 found a low level of compliance by the Chinese government regarding the obligations it assumed in the 1992 MOU and the 1994 SOC. [30]

Extensive evidence indicates products from China's prison labor system are exported to other countries, including the United States. A U.S. diplomatic cable from May 2008 specifically identifies artificial flowers, Christmas lights, shoes, garments, and umbrellas as products allegedly produced in Chinese prison factories for middlemen companies, which subsequently market them with the presumed possibility of export. [31] The U.S. Department of Labor's 2013 report on forced labor products adds to this list coal, cotton, electronics,

---

laws ... Congress urges the [PRC] to allow international inspections of places of detention that are suspected of producing export goods in order to ensure that such production does not take place..." U.S. Congress Concurrent Resolution 105, Stat. 2441, "China-Human Rights Violations" (H. Con. Res. 216), Nov. 21, 1991.

[11] For examples of the role of prison labor in the debate over granting MFN to China, see *Bloomberg Business News*, "China Prison Tapes Again Part of MFN Debate," May 19, 1994; and Elizabeth Perry, "Most Favored Nation Status and the Political Potential of Chinese Labor," Center for Labor Studies, University of Washington (1995), *http://depts.washington.edu/pcls/documents/research/Perry_MostFavoredNation.pdf*. For an example of discussions of prison labor as it related to China's entry into the WTO, see speeches on the floor of the U.S. Senate by Senator Paul Wellstone and Senator Frank Lautenberg, as contained in Congressional Record, vol. 147 (September 12, 2000), pp. S175582-84.

[12] For the text of these documents, see Appendices 2 and 3 of this report; and for more detailed discussion on issues surrounding the MOU and SOC, see U.S.-China Economic and Security Review Commission, *2008 Annual Report to Congress,* November 2008, pp. 317-332.

[13] The full legislative mandate of the U.S.-China Economic and Security Review Commission is available at the Commission's website on the "Charter" webpage. *http://www.uscc.gov /about/charter.php.*

fireworks, footwear, garments, nails, and toys, though it does not provide details on which prison-made products might be exported abroad. [32][14]

Furthermore, several allegations have been made in recent years regarding the export or attempted export of Chinese prison-made goods, including the following:

- Li Guirong, a former prisoner who served two separate terms from December 2001 to December 2002 and June 2004 to December 2005 in the Heizuizi RTL Camp for Women (Jilin Province) for offenses of "disturbing public order," claimed the inmates at Heizuizi worked shifts of up to 20 hours manufacturing cloth paste (a raw material used in the dyeing of textiles) for export to Japan. [33]
- John Sims, a British citizen imprisoned in a facility in Ningbo (Zhejiang Province) in 2006, claimed that he and other prisoners were forced to manufacture Coca Cola-themed Christmas ornaments intended for export sale. Coca Cola stated it found "no evidence" of prison labor production in the matter but terminated its business relationship with the Chinese supplier in question. [34] Coca Cola further asserted its policies "expressly prohibit the use of all forms of forced labor, including prison labor" in the production of company merchandise. [35]
- A report published by the Laogai Research Foundation revealed the use by 120 Chinese prison enterprises of English-language, on-line marketing targeting international clients. One such example was the 2009 confirmed use of *China Commodity Net*, a Ministry of Commerce-sponsored website, by Yunnan Jinma Mining and Machinery Works – the commercial identity of the Yunnan No. 2 Prison – to post English advertisements for the intended sale abroad of "belt conveyors," "tramcars," "auto spoke plates," and "high-efficiency tank type multi-purpose pulverizers." [36]
- Danny Cancian, a New Zealand citizen incarcerated in Dongguan Prison (Guangdong Province) from 2009 to 2012, alleged he and other prisoners were forced to make disposable headphones for Airphonics,

---

[14] The Department of Labor (DoL) does not maintain databases of specific companies suspected of marketing these goods, for either Chinese domestic or international consumption. DoL personnel have indicated they do not have adequate resources to perform detailed and on-going research of this nature, and that performing field research inside China would be extremely difficult. Discussions between Commission staff and representatives of the DoL's Bureau of International Labor Affairs, June 6, 2012.

a Taiwan-based company that sells the headsets to commercial airlines, including Qantas, British Airways, and Emirates. Mr. Cancian also claimed the prisoners made inductors for use in electrical appliances, which were sold to a local company that in turn provided them to foreign companies, including Electrolux and Emerson. [37] Some of the companies named have rejected these claims: Electrolux, for example, issued a statement that an internal company inquiry revealed "[n]o information ... to indicate that components from [Dongguan] prison were incorporated into Electrolux products." [38]

- From 2012 to 2013, Falun Gong practitioners made specific and detailed allegations of forced labor export production at multiple facilities in China. Practitioners claimed the Hebei Province Women's Prison was producing a range of towels, diapers, and cloth products for the Hebei Yikang Knitting And Cotton Co., Ltd., which then was marketing these products internationally. [39] Falun Gong practitioners also charged the Inner Mongolia Women's Prison, operating under a dual identity as the Yinghua Garment Factory, with producing textiles, chopsticks, and buckwheat for export. [40]

- In September 2012, a woman in New York City found a letter in a Saks Fifth Avenue shopping bag written by a man claiming to be incarcerated in a Chinese prison labor facility. The letter was signed "Tohnain Emmanuel Njong" and accompanied by a small photo of a man in an orange jacket. Later found and interviewed, Njong, a citizen of Cameroon, said he was an English teacher in Shenzhen (Guangdong Province), when in May 2011 he was unjustly convicted of fraud and sentenced to a prison labor camp. According to Njong, he was forced to work 13 hours per day making paper bags, assembling electronics, or sewing garments, with no outside contact, until he was released in December 2013 for good behavior.

    The letter's discovery in 2012 led to investigations by the Laogai Research Foundation and U.S. Department of Homeland Security (DHS). Saks Fifth Avenue and its affiliate, Hudson Bay Company, claim to be verifying the companies' strict labor policies throughout their global supply chains for evidence of prison-made products. [41]

- Stuart Foster, a U.S. citizen convicted of theft in April 2013 while teaching at the Guangdong University of Foreign Studies, was sentenced to the Baiyun Detention Center in Guangzhou (Guangdong Province) for eight months. Foster claimed he was forced under threat of physical punishment to work more than eight hours a day, six days a week assembling Christmas lights intended for export to the United States and other western countries. [42]

- Allegations of "gold farming"[15] in Chinese prison labor facilities emerged in a 2011 story published by *The Guardian*. A former prisoner using the pseudonym Liu Dali claimed he was sentenced in 2004 to three years of RTL in a camp in Jixi (Heilongjiang Province)[16] for "illegally petitioning" central government officials about corruption in his local area. In addition to performing work digging in open-trench coal mines, carving chopsticks, and assembling automotive seat covers (intended for export to South Korea and Japan), Liu described a system in which prisoners were forced to spend 12-hour shifts in the evenings playing online games to build up virtual credits that were then sold online by camp officials. [43] According to Liu, prison officials made approximately $785–$940 per day from the "gold farming" services performed by prisoners, which made the work more profitable than the prison's more traditional manufacturing enterprises. No compensation was provided to the prisoners themselves. [44] Although playing computer

---

[15] Gold farming (also termed "powerleveling") is a practice associated with many online role-playing games, in which a player pays someone else to play their character for them – thereby building up points that make their characters more powerful or acquiring possessions (e.g., wealth, weapons) that similarly make them stronger. Online vendors may also offer for sale existing characters whose power and wealth have already been built up through extended periods of game play, or virtual goods that can be transferred to other characters. Vili Lehdonvirta and Mirko Ernkvist, *Knowledge Map of the Virtual Economy: Converting the Virtual Economy into Development Potential* (The International Bank for Reconstruction and Development, The World Bank, April 2011), pp. 7-9. *http://www.infodev.org/infodev-files/resource/InfodevDocuments_1076.pdf*. Websites acting as brokers for such trades are easily locatable online. On August 6, 2012, Commission staff located (with a single Google search) the website *www.ogdeal.com*, which claims the title of "The Leading MMORPG ('massively multiplayer online role-playing game') Services Company." The site offered credit exchanges for over 40 popular online games (to include *Anarchy, Age of Conan, Diablo 3, Final Fantasy, Warhammer, Star Wars: The Old Republic*, etc.), with payments "via Paypal, Moneybookers, Libertyreserve [sic] and Westernunion [sic] within 10mins after the trade." "Sell Anarchy Online Credits," *www.ogdeal.com. http://www.ogdeal.com/sell-anarchy-online.html*.

[16] In media accounts of this case, "Liu Dali" described his detention facility as an RTL camp in the city of Jixi. The Laogai Research Foundation identifies two prison labor facilities in Jixi: (1) the "Jixi Prison" and (2) the "Jixi Reeducation Through Labor" Facility. The Jixi Prison is listed as heavily engaged in coal mining and production of handicrafts; the Jixi RTL is identified as a former center for coal mining, and current manufacturing facility for plastic bags. Laogai Research Foundation, *Laogai Handbook 2007-2008* (Washington, DC, 2008), pp. 166 and 178. Assuming that Liu Dali is truthful, it is unclear as to which facility his account refers.

games might seem to be a relatively benign form of forced labor, Liu claimed prisoners who failed to earn the required numbers of virtual credits would be beaten by prison guards: "If I couldn't complete my work quota, they would punish me physically. They would make me stand with my hands raised in the air and after I returned to my dormitory they would beat me with plastic pipes. We kept playing until we could barely see things." [45]

The allegations of forced "gold farming" carry new and potentially significant implications for U.S. policies and laws pertaining to prison labor products. If virtual goods generated by prisoners can be offered for sale online, prisoners also could be used for other repetitive and low-skill online tasks, such as spamming, "cherry blossoming,"[17] or "click fraud."[18] U.S. laws pertaining to the import of forced labor products have not caught up with such information age innovations.

Masanjia "Reeducation Through Labor" Camp

The most detailed accounts of Chinese prison export production – and of prisoner abuse – to emerge in 2013 involved the Masanjia RTL Facility, located outside Shenyang (Liaoning Province).

---

[17] "'Cherry blossoming' is a term used ... to refer to small marketing related digital tasks, such as 'liking' a brand's Facebook page against a small pay. It resembles microwork in that it involves recruiting large numbers of workers to complete small tasks for a business client." Cherry blossoming could also be used to increase the number of hits on a company or product webpage, thereby raising its Internet profile and seeming popularity with consumers. Vili Lehdonvirta & Mirko Ernkvist, *Knowledge Map of the Virtual Economy: Converting the Virtual Economy into Development Potential* (Washington, DC: The International Bank for Reconstruction and Development/The World Bank, 2011), p. 7. *http://www.infodev.org/infodev-files/resource/InfodevDocuments_1056.pdf.*

[18] Click fraud is believed to be a widespread phenomenon in China. According to *PC Magazine Online*, click fraud is the practice of "[c]licking ad banners without any intention of purchasing the product. Click fraud is done to make an ad campaign appear more effective. Paying a few cents per hour to workers in a third-world country to sit at a computer all day and do nothing but click banners makes an ad campaign appear very successful. If ads are based on click-throughs (pay-per-click), the Web site publishing the ads and clicking the ads countless times can make a dishonest profit." *PC Magazine Online*, "Definition of: click fraud." *http://www.pcmag.com/encyclopedia_term/0%2C1237%2Ct%3 Dclick+fraud &i%3D39774%2C00.asp;* John Leyden, "Chinese Mobile Malware Powers Click-Fraud Scam," *The Register*, February 17, 2011; and Erick Schonfeld, "The Evolution of Click Fraud: Massive Chinese Operation 'DormRing1' Uncovered," *TechCrunch.com*, October 8, 2009. *http://techcrunch.com/2009/10/08/the-evolution-of-click-fraud-massive-chinese-operation-dormring1-uncovered/.*

Inquiries into conditions at the facility began in October 2012 when a woman in Portland, Oregon, discovered a letter inside a box of Halloween decorations purportedly written by an anonymous prisoner at the Masanjia site (see Figure 2). The letter described harsh working conditions and brutal treatment at the hands of prison authorities. [46] [19]

The resulting publicity led the Chinese magazine *Lens* to produce an investigative article on the women's prison at Masanjia. [47] This was followed by the release of *Above the Ghosts' Heads: The Women of Masanjia Labour Camp*, a Chinese-language documentary film that employed accounts from former prisoners to reveal conditions at the facility. The central source for both the article and the film is Liu Hua, a middle-aged farmer who claimed she and her husband were charged with "endangering state security" and "opposing socialism" after exposing corruption by their village's Party secretary, and sentenced to three years of RTL at Masanjia. Despite Masanjia prison regulations that forbid inmates from having writing materials, Liu kept a secret journal of her experiences as a prisoner. In the film, she describes brutal working conditions, torture of inmates, and corruption among prison officials. [48]

The women's prison at Masanjia functions in part as a garment factory, producing uniforms for the People's Armed Police. It operates under a commercial identity as the "Xinyu Clothing Company"[20] producing clothing, such as shirts for a South Korean company and down-filled cotton jackets for export to Italy.

Workers who failed to meet work quotas or comply with regulations were subject to beatings, and Liu claims that she herself was severely beaten on the instructions of prison officials. [49]

---

[19] Journalists in China working for CNN later made contact with a man who claimed to be the writer of the letter; this "Mr. Zhang" told CNN that he was an adherent of Falun Gong, who was arrested in the lead-up to the 2008 Beijing Olympics and sentenced to two and a half years of confinement at Masanjia. Steven Jiang, "Chinese Labor Camp Inmate Tells of True Horror of Halloween 'SOS'," *CNN Online*, November 7, 2013. *http://www.cnn.com/2013/11/06/world/asia/china-labor-camp-halloween-sos/index.html?hpt=hp_c2.*

[20] In addition to Liu Hua's account, an online company profile of the Xinyu Garment Company states that "We welcome all new and old customers to visit ... Our specific address is: Shenyang City, Yuhong District, Masanjia North Township (Liaoning Province Reeducation Through Labor Facility)." Xinyu Clothing Company, Ltd., *czvv.com* (Chinese language business directory website). Translation by Authors. *http://3533576.czvv.com/about* .

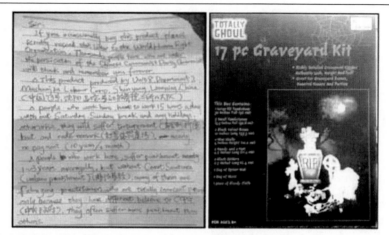

Image left: The letter discovered in October 2012 by a woman in Portland, Oregon, in which the anonymous writer described harsh conditions in the Masanjia RTL Facility. Andrew Jacobs, "Behind Cry for Help from China Labor Camp," *New York Times*, June 11, 2013. *http://www.nytimes.com/2013 /06/12/world/asia/man-details-risks-in-exposing-chinas-forced-labor.html.*

Image right: The box of Halloween decorations – purchased at a local K-Mart retail store – in which the letter was discovered. Rachel Stark, "Halloween Decorations Carry Haunting Message of Forced Labor," *Oregonian*, December 23, 2012. *http://www.oregonlive.com/happy-valley/index.ssf/2012 /12/halloweendecorationscarryha.html.*

Figure 2. Alleged Forced Labor Products from the Masanjia Prison Facility.

The reports on conditions at Masanjia prompted varying reactions by Chinese authorities. Chinese censors delayed publication of the May 2013 issue of *Lens* magazine and placed controls on the magazine, and police officials reportedly harassed former prisoners identified in the piece. [50] The documentary was banned in China but has circulated on the Internet, [51] and the *Lens* article is no longer available online. Chinese state media have denied the allegations of abuse at Masanjia, defending the facility's "many years of upholding the Party's [RTL] work policies ... transforming many members of the 'Falun Gong' cult ... and upholding social stability." [52] In May 2013, the lead filmmaker for the project, Du Bin, was detained in Beijing on public order offenses – likely resulting from his work on the film and publication in Hong Kong the previous week of a book on what he referred to as the 1989 "Tiananmen massacre." His current status and whereabouts are unknown. [53]

Policy Response and Enforcement Efforts by U.S. Government Agencies

Legal prohibitions against importing prison labor products into the United States historically have had a weak record of enforcement, due to the requirement that U.S. law enforcement authorities must acquire "credible, first-hand knowledge ... that suspected goods are produced with prison, slave, or forced labor in order to prohibit their entry into the United States." [54] However, this first-hand knowledge typically must come from Chinese citizens, who almost certainly would face retribution from the Chinese government for providing testimony to a foreign government. This severely limits the ability of U.S. enforcement authorities to obtain conclusive evidence. [55]

Among U.S. government agencies, DHS bears primary responsibility for policy and enforcement issues related to the importation of goods produced by prison labor.

Immigration and Customs Enforcement (ICE) coordinates investigations into the illegal importation of forced labor products, treating such cases as a form of commercial fraud. [56] In investigating such cases, ICE works in close coordination with U.S. Customs and Border Protection, which bears responsibility for detaining or seizing any suspected or confirmed shipments of prison labor products at U.S. ports of entry, as well as issuing withhold release orders in applicable circumstances. [57]

To pursue investigations in China, ICE depends on five special agents, four working in Beijing, and one working in Guangzhou. [58] However, ICE faces competing priorities from a "myriad of crimes ranging from money laundering, child pornography, strategic weapons [proliferation] ... [and] human trafficking," and has been unable to devote its full resources to stopping prison labor imports. [59] Furthermore, in regards to prison labor issues, ICE personnel working in China have experienced a systemic lack of cooperation from their interlocutors in the PRC Ministry of Justice. [60]

ICE officials currently have 12 outstanding cases involving suspected export production prisons in China–including the most recent, a November 2012 inquiry opened on the Masanjia facility–but have experienced minimal cooperation from Chinese officials in resolving these cases. [61]

UPDATE: Luzhong Prison and Site Visits under Terms of the 1994 Statement of Cooperation

In its *2008 Annual Report to Congress*, the Commission profiled the legal case of Marck & Associates, Inc. v. Photo USA Corporation.[21] Marck & Associates, Inc. (hereafter "Marck") and Photo USA Corporation are competitors in the market for drinkware products such as ceramic coffee mugs. Marck filed a lawsuit against Photo USA in the Federal District Court for the Northern District of Ohio, alleging, among other unfair business practices, the defendant was acting as a wholesaler and distributor of coffee mugs purchased from Shandong Zibo Maolong Ceramics Company, a front company for the Luzhong Prison (Shandong Province). The court ruled that Marck failed to meet the necessary evidentiary burden to establish that Photo USA's products were produced by prison labor. [62]

On May 11, 2009, officials from the U.S. Embassy in Beijing were allowed to inspect the Luzhong Prison facility – the first time since 2006 that a site visit was permitted under the terms of the 1992 MOU and 1994 SOC. The visiting U.S. officials reported no signs of ceramics manufacturing at the site, and that prison officials told them "the prison conducted cement manufacturing and coal mining operations in the past and now produces plastic packaging, primarily for nearby chemical companies." Embassy officials also met with the director of the Shandong Zibo Maolong Ceramics Company (located adjacent to the prison), who stated the company was a private enterprise with no ties to the prison. Based on the visit, ICE decided to close its case file on the facility. [63]

Plaintiff's counsel in the *Marck v. Photo USA* case claimed ceramic production at Luzhong had decreased, or ceased entirely, by mid-2008 due to publicity surrounding the lawsuit. [64]

While this assertion cannot be independently confirmed, the lengthy delays in allowing prison site visits – if requested visits ever occur at all – have shown the 1994 SOC to be an inefficient tool for resolving U.S. concerns regarding Chinese prison export production facilities.

---

[21] As stated in the Commission's *2008 Annual Report to Congress*, the Commission takes no position on the litigation between Marck and Photo USA, makes no judgment regarding the veracity of particular claims by either side, and does not seek to influence the outcome of this litigation in any way. The Commission's sole interest in this case lies in its illustrative value for public policy debates surrounding the alleged importation into the United States of products produced in China by forced labor.

The Luzhong Prison inspection illustrates continuing non-compliance by Chinese officials with the terms of the 1992 MOU and 1994 SOC. Per the latter agreement, visits to suspect facilities are to be arranged within 60 days of the receipt of any such request; however, testimony before the Commission in 2008 indicated 13 outstanding visit requests by U.S. officials, dating back to 1994. As of July 2014, there are 7 outstanding requests. [65] In the case of Luzhong Prison, ICE officials made initial inquiries regarding the facility beginning in 2006, [66] and issued the first of a series of formal requests to visit the site in October 2007. [67]

PROSPECTS FOR REFORM OF THE "REEDUCATION THROUGH LABOR" SYSTEM

Under PRC statutory law, it is illegal for prison labor products to be exported abroad.[22] Unfortunately, competing interests at the local, provincial, and national level within the party-state bureaucracy reduce enforcement and cooperation within the context of the MOU. In one past case, Chinese government economic and trade officials "concurred [with U.S. embassy officials] that 'reeducation through labor' facilities were covered by the MOU and ... indicated they would try to persuade the Ministry of Justice to grant ... access" for investigation. [68] It is also likely, as with their U.S. counterparts, Chinese entities tasked with enforcing the non-export of prison labor products experience many competing priorities and lack the institutional capacity at the central level to prevent their export effectively.

A recent reform to the prison labor system, if truly implemented, could substantially reduce the number of laborers forced to produce goods for export. Following the Third Plenum of the 18th CCP Central Committee in November 2013, the Chinese government announced it would abolish the RTL program. [69] On December 28, 2013, the National People's Congress repealed laws and regulations relating to RTL. [70]

---

[22] "China prohibits export of products made with prison labour. No competent Chinese authorities [have] ever given any reform-through-labour unit the right to export commodities... [t]he Chinese Government is very strict on this point and any violations of these regulations are dealt with severely." Information Office of the State Council of the People's Republic of China, "Reform of Criminals through Labour," Government White Paper: Criminal Reform in China, Part 3, August 1992. http://www.china.org.cn/e-white/criminal/8-4.htm.

China's new leadership likely seeks to be seen as responding to public outrage over a string of high-profile abuses that have been covered extensively in recent years in official and unofficial media in China and discussed by Chinese Internet users.

- According to an October 2012 commentary from Xinhua, the Chinese government's official news agency, "[m]any cases have shown that the labor re-education system has been misused to persecute innocent people and illegally punish protestors. The system has infringed on human rights and the rule of law, undermining the government's accountability." [71]
- A December 2013 article published by *China Daily,* an official Chinese news source, profiled multiple people who had suffered under the RTL system from its earliest years, and noted how the system conflicted with provisions of the PRC Constitution. [72]
- Nationwide public outcry against the RTL sentence of Ren Jianyu, a village official in the southwest of Chongqing Municipality, for "spreading negative information and inciting the subversion of state power" caused the local committee to revoke the sentence halfway through his detention. He was released in November 2012. [73]

Chinese leaders also likely aim to be seen as improving the rule of law at the local level after officials like Bo Xilai, former Chongqing party chief (since imprisoned for life on corruption charges), was exposed in 2012 for misusing RTL to target his critics. [74] [23]

The announcement to eliminate RTL has already resulted in the release of many prisoners. Reports less than two months following the abolishment of RTL indicate tens of thousands of prisoners have been released. [75]

Chinese and Western human rights activists and legal scholars welcomed news of the policy change but expressed doubts regarding the extent of future reform. [76]

Pilot programs for RTL reform, launched in 2011 and 2012 in various cities, [24] may help illuminate China's ultimate plans for RTL reform. These

---

[23] From 2009 to 2012, Bo seized more than $11 billion in illicit funds and made "heavy use ... of measures that allow[ed] police to lock [more than 5,700] people away without trial." Stanley Lubman, "Bo Xilai's Gift to Chongqing: A Legal Mess," *Wall Street Journal,* April 12, 2012. *http://blogs.*

[24] In late 2012, Chinese officials launched pilot projects in four cities – Jinan, Lanzhou, Nanjing, and Zhengzhou – to study possible reform measures. Earlier that year, pilot projects began in the four cities in Shandong, Gansu, Jiangsu, and Henan provinces. At the same time,

pilot programs have centered on resolving the dispute between the police and judiciary bodies over which organization has the ultimate decision-making authority in administering RTL sentences. [77] The limited information available regarding these pilot programs indicates reforms could to some extent reduce police authority in reviewing and approving RTL cases.

Other reports of institutional changes to RTL include re-designating RTL facilities as drug treatment centers, presumably where non-violent drug offenders would continue to be detained, without legal due process, under forced labor conditions and expanding "community correction programs." [78] Furthermore, China's State Council reportedly approved reorganizing the Beijing Bureau of RTL Administration as the Bureau of Educational Correction under the auspices of the Ministry of Justice. Experts familiar with this development assess this specific revision "reflects a deepening of the administrative examination and approval system and strengthening the establishment of a service-oriented government model."

If effectively implemented, the elimination of RTL would remove the major tool used by local officials to arbitrarily imprison Chinese citizens and represent a significant step forward for both human rights and the development of China's criminal justice system. However, even if China abolishes RTL, local governments likely will retain methods to detain government critics, either extralegally – such as confinement in "black jails" or psychiatric hospitals – or through the current legal system. Local governments also may have economic incentives to continue operating RTL facilities despite central government directives.

Finally, continuing concerns about the ripple effect of the marked increase in domestic protests since 2012, recurrent ethnic unrest in Tibet and Xinjiang, and the "Arab Spring" triggered in late 2010, may encourage officials at every level to use abusive control tools to prevent activities and dissidents from creating disturbances. [79] This could prevent any meaningful reform on civil and political rights, regardless of the scope of RTL reform.

---

several areas, including Chongqing and Heilongjiang, initiated "pilot projects and adjustments of their own, but even these 'corrections' are based on provisions in relevant [existing] laws." Dui Hua Foundation, "RTL: Reporters Shed Some Light on Reform Projects," December 11, 2012. *http://www.duihuahrjournal.org/2012/12/rtl-reporters*

APPENDIX 1: U.S. GOVERNMENT LEGAL PROHIBITIONS ON THE IMPORTATION OF PRISON LABOR PRODUCTS

Section 307 of the Tariff Act of 1930 (commonly known as the "Smoot-Hawley Tariff Act") makes it illegal to import goods into the United States produced by prison labor. The law explicitly prohibits the importation of "all goods, wares, articles and merchandise mined, produced, or manufactured wholly or in part in any foreign country by convict labor or/and forced labor or/and indentured labor under penal sanctions." [80]

Text from the Tariff Act of 1930 emphasizes that *forced labor* is central to the law's intent: "'Forced labor,' as herein used, shall mean all work or service which is exacted from any person under the menace of any penalty for its nonperformance and for which the worker does not offer himself voluntarily." [81]

Furthermore, Section 1761 of Title 18 of the U.S. Code states that "[w]hoever knowingly transports ... from any foreign country into the United States any goods, wares, or merchandise manufactured, produced, or mined, wholly or in part by convicts or prisoners ... or in any penal or reformatory institution," may be subject to fines or imprisonment up to two years. [82]

The United States is also a signatory to Convention #105 of the International Labor Organization (an agency of the United Nations), which requires member states "to suppress and not to make use of any form of forced or compulsory labour" for the purposes "of political coercion or education or as a punishment for holding or expressing political views or views ideologically opposed to the established political, social or economic system" or "as a method of mobilising and using labour for purposes of economic development."[25]

There have been steps proposed in recent years to update existing U.S. laws on prison labor products. For example, legislation entitled the Customs Facilitation and Trade Enforcement Reauthorization Act of 2009, co-sponsored by then chairman of the Senate Finance Committee, Senator Max Baucus (D-MT) and Ranking Member Charles Grassley (R-IA), would have expanded the language of Section 307 by also banning any imports produced "by means of coercion" and/or by "individuals ... subjected to a severe form of

---

[25] The United States ratified Convention #105 in September 1991; the PRC is not a signatory. International Labour Organization, "C105 - Abolition of Forced Labour Convention, 1957 (No. 105) – Convention Concerning the Abolition of Forced Labour" (entered into force: January 17, 1959). *http://www.ilo.org/dyn/normlex/en/f?p=NORMLEXPUB: 12100:0:: NO:12100:P12100_INSTRUMENT_ID:312250: NO.*

trafficking in persons." The bill would also have tasked U.S. Immigration and Customs Enforcement to "prepare and publish" in the *Federal Register* "the name and country of each producer of goods the importation of which is prohibited" under U.S. law.[26]

Some U.S. trade associations reportedly expressed concerns over the bill on multiple grounds, to include: questioning the accuracy and currency of information on forced labor production held by U.S. government agencies; concern that all sourcing from a given country could be called into question if instances of forced/prison labor production for export were to be identified in that country; and that it might lead to "a 'slippery slope' problem where this definition could be continually expanded, [creating] uncertainty in terms of how the expanded definition would play out when it comes to enforcement." [83] However, this bill was not passed, [84] and the original text of Section 307 of the Tariff Act of 1930 remains in effect.

APPENDIX 2: TEXT OF THE 1992 U.S.-CHINA MEMORANDUM OF UNDERSTANDING REGARDING THE PROHIBITION OF IMPORT AND EXPORT TRADE IN PRISON LABOR PRODUCTS

MEMORANDUM OF UNDERSTANDING BETWEEN THE UNITED STATES OF AMERICA AND THE PEOPLE'S REPUBLIC OF CHINA ON PROHIBITING IMPORT AND EXPORT TRADE IN PRISON LABOR PRODUCTS

The Government of the United States of America and the Government of the People's Republic of China (hereinafter referred to as the Parties),

Considering that the Chinese Government has noted and respects United States laws and regulations that prohibit the import of prison labor products,

---

[26] "Prohibition on Importation - No good may be imported into the United States, if that good was produced, in whole or in part - (1) with convict labor, forced labor, or indentured labor under penal sanctions; (2) by means of coercion (as defined in Section 103 of the Trafficking Victims Protection Act of 2000 (22 U.S.C. 7102)), including by means of an employer withholding the passport or other travel documents of a foreign worker in order to compel the production of that good; or (3) by 1 or more individuals who, at the time of the production were being subjected to a severe form of trafficking in persons (as defined in Section 103 of the Trafficking Victims Protection Act of 2000 (22 U.S.C. 7102))." *Customs Facilitation and Trade Enforcement Reauthorization Act of 2009* (S.1631.IS), draft language for "Sec. 308," introduced August 6, 2009 (111th Cong., 2009–2010). *http://thomas.loc.gov/cgibin/query*

has consistently paid great attention to the question of prohibition of the export of prison labor products, has explained to the United States its policy on this question, and on October 10, 1991, reiterated its regulations regarding prohibition of the export of prison labor products;

Considering that the Government of the United States has explained to the Chinese Government U.S. laws and regulations prohibiting the import of prison labor products and the policy of the United States on this issue; and

Noting that both Governments express appreciation for each other's concerns and previous efforts to resolve this issue,

Have reached the following understanding on the question of prohibiting import and export trade between the two countries that violates the relevant laws and regulations of either the United States or China concerning products produced by prison or penal labor (herein referred to as prison labor products).

The Parties agree:

1) Upon the request of one Party, and based on specific information provided by that Party, the other Party will promptly investigate companies, enterprises or units suspected of violating relevant regulations and laws, and will immediately report the results of such investigations to the other.

2) Upon the request of one Party, responsible officials or experts of relevant departments of both Parties will meet under mutually convenient circumstances to exchange information on the enforcement of relevant laws and regulations and to examine and report on compliance with relevant regulations and laws by their respective companies, enterprises, or units.

3) Upon request, each Party will furnish to the other Party available evidence and information regarding suspected violations of relevant laws and regulations in a form admissible in judicial or administrative proceedings of the other Party. Moreover, at the request of one Party, the other Party will preserve the confidentiality of the furnished evidence, except when used in judicial or administrative proceedings.

4) In order to resolve specific outstanding cases related to the subject matter of this Memorandum of Understanding, each Party will, upon request of the other Party, promptly arrange and facilitate visits by responsible officials of the other Party's diplomatic mission to its respective companies, enterprises or units.

This Memorandum of Understanding will enter into force upon signature.

DONE at Washington, in duplicate, this seventh day of August, 1992, in the English and the Chinese languages, both texts being equally authentic.

FOR THE GOVERNMENT OF THE
UNITED STATES OF AMERICA:

FOR THE GOVERNMENT OF THE
PEOPLE'S REPUBLIC OF CHINA:

APPENDIX 3: TEXT OF THE 1994 U.S.-CHINA STATEMENT OF COOPERATION REGARDING THE PROHIBITION OF IMPORT AND EXPORT TRADE IN PRISON LABOR PRODUCTS

STATEMENT OF COOPERATION ON THE IMPLEMENTATION OF THE MEMORANDUM OF UNDERSTANDING BETWEEN THE UNITED STATES OF AMERICA AND THE PEOPLE'S REPUBLIC OF CHINA ON PROHIBITING IMPORT AND EXPORT TRADE IN PRISON LABOR PRODUCTS

1) Summary: The statement of cooperation on implementation of the prison labor MOU was signed at 09:00 LT in Beijing March 14, 1994. Ministry of Justice Reform Through Labor Bureau Director - General Wang Mingdi signed for the Chinese side, Econ Mincouns Szymanski signed for the U.S. side. This message contains the final text of the document as signed and a background document distributed at Secretary Christopher's press conference where the signing of the document was announced. End Summary.

2) Final text of the statement of cooperation on implementation of the prison labor MOU, signed at 09:00 LT in Beijing March 14, 1994 follows:

BEGIN TEXT

As the Chinese government acknowledges and respects United States laws concerning the prohibition of the import of prison labor products, and the

United States government recognizes and respects Chinese legal regulations concerning the prohibition of the export of prison labor products;

As China and the United States take note and appreciate the good intentions and efforts made by both sides in implementing the "Memorandum of Understanding" signed in August 1992;

The Chinese government and the United States government agree that conducting investigations of suspected exports of prison labor products destined for the United States requires cooperation between both sides in order to assure the enforcement of the relevant laws of both countries. Both sides agree that they should stipulate clear guidelines and procedures for the conduct of these investigations. Therefore, both sides agree to the establishment of specialized procedures and guidelines according to the following provisions:

First, when one side provides the other side a request, based on specific information, to conduct investigations of suspected exports of prison labor products destined for the United States, the receiving side will provide the requesting side a comprehensive investigative report within 60 days of the receipt of said written request. At the same time, the requesting side will provide a concluding evaluation of the receiving side's investigative report within 60 days of receipt of the report.

Second, if the United States government, in order to resolve specific outstanding cases, requests a visit to a suspected facility, the Chinese government will, in conformity with Chinese laws and regulations and in accordance with the MOU, arrange for responsible United States diplomatic mission officials to visit the suspected facility within 60 days of the receipt of a written request.

Third, the United States government will submit a report indicating the results of the visit to the Chinese government within 60 days of a visit by diplomatic officials to a suspected facility.

Fourth, in cases where the U.S. government presents new or previously unknown information on suspected exports of prison labor products destined for the U.S. regarding a suspected facility that was already visited, the Chinese government will organize new investigations and notify the U.S. side. If necessary, it can also be arranged for the U.S. side to again visit that suspected facility.

Fifth, when the Chinese government organizes the investigation of a suspected facility and the U.S. side is allowed to visit the suspected facility, the U.S. side will provide related information conducive to the investigation. In order to accomplish the purpose of the visit, the Chinese side will, in accordance with its laws and regulations, provide an opportunity to consult relevant records and materials on-site and arrange visits to necessary areas of the facility.

The U.S. side agrees to protect relevant proprietary information of customers of the facility consistent with the relevant terms of the prison labor MOU.

Sixth, both sides agree that arrangements for U.S. diplomats to visit suspected facilities, in principle, will proceed after the visit to a previous suspected facility is completely ended and a report indicating the results of the visit is submitted.

Both sides further agree to continue to strengthen already established effective contacts between the concerned ministries of the Chinese government and the U.S. Embassy in Beijing and to arrange meetings to discuss specific details when necessary to further the implementation of the MOU in accordance with the points noted above.

Done at Beijing, in duplicate, this Thirteenth day of March, 1992, in the English and the Chinese languages, both texts being equally authentic.

Representative
of the Chinese side:
Wang Mingdi

Representative
of the United States side:
Christopher J. Szymanski

3. The statement of cooperation was signed, for the Chinese side by Ministry of Justice Reform Through Labor Bureau Director – General Wang Mingdi and for the U.S. side by Econ Mincouns Christopher J. Szymanski.

4. Secretary Christopher announced the signing of the statement at a 10:45 LT press conference in Beijing. The text of a background document distributed at the Secretary's press conference follows:

BEGIN TEXT

The original Memorandum of Understanding on prohibiting import and export trade in prison labor products, signed in Washington August 7, 1992, provides for cases of suspected exports of prison-made goods to the U.S. to be referred to the Chinese government for investigation and, if necessary, for U.S. officials to conduct visits to the suspected facilities.

In the first year of implementation it became apparent that explicit implementation guidelines needed to be developed.

In January 1994, in an exchange of letters with the Chinese side, we determined general guidelines for implementation to be used as a basis for the development of a "Statement of Cooperation".

The "Statement of Cooperation" signed this morning sets out working-level procedures to be followed by both sides and delineates objective standards for assessing bilateral implementation. These include:

- Investigations of suspected exports, requested by one side, will be concluded and reported by the other side within sixty days of request.
- A written evaluation of the investigative report will be submitted by the requesting side within sixty days after receipt of the report.
- Requested visits to suspected facilities will be arranged by the Chinese side within sixty days of request.
- The U.S. side will provide a visit report to the Chinese side within sixty days of the visit.
- If new information is provided by the U.S. concerning a previously visited facility, the Chinese side will reinvestigate and, if necessary, arrange a second visit.
- During visits to suspected facilities, the Chinese will provide an opportunity for U.S. officials to consult records and materials on-site and visit relevant areas of the facility.
- Visits to other suspected facilities will be arranged following the provision by the U.S. side of a report of previous visits.

REFERENCES

[1]   U.S. Senate Committee on Foreign Relations, Hearing on the U.S. Implementation of Prison Labor Agreements with China, testimony of Jeffrey Bader, May 21, 1997. http://www.gpo.gov/fdsys/pkg/CHRG-105shrg47725/pdf/CHRG-105shrg47725.pdf; and U.S. Immigration and Customs Enforcement official (U.S. Department of Homeland Security), email interview with Commission staff, April 14, 2014.

[2]   U.S.-China Economic and Security Review Commission, 2008 Annual Report to Congress, November 2008, pp. 317-332.

[3]   Ramin Pejan, Laogai: "Reform Through Labor" in China (Human Rights Brief, 2000), p. 1. http://www.wcl.american.edu/hrbrief/07/2laogai.cfm.

[4]   Michael Pareles, "Hard Times and Hard Labor: Prison Labor Reform in China from 1978 to the Present," Greater China (Winter 2006). http://www.stanford.edu/group/sjeaa/journal61/china3.pdf.

[5]   Human Rights in China, State Secrets: China's Legal Labyrinth, (June 2007),   p.13.   http://www.hrichina.org/sites/default/files/PDFs/State-Secrets-Report/HRIC_StateSecrets-Report.pdf.

[6]   Congressional-Executive Commission on China, Roundtable on Forced Labor in China, testimony of Harry Wu, June 22, 2005; and Laogai Research Foundation, "What Is The Laogai System?" http://www. laogai.org/page/whatlaogai-system.

[7]   U.S.-China Economic and Security Review Commission, 2008 Annual Report to Congress, November 2008, p. 320; and Congressional-Executive Commission on China, Annual Report 2013, October 10, 2013, p. 158.

[8]   Philip Williams, The Great Wall of Confinement: The Chinese Prison Camp Through Contemporary Fiction and Reportage (Berkeley, CA: University of California Press, 2004), pp. 58-60; and James Seymour and Richard Anderson, New Ghosts, Old Ghosts: Prisons and Labor Reform Camps in China (Armonk, NY: M.E. Sharpe, 1999), pp. 190-198.

[9]   Congressional-Executive Commission on China, Annual Report 2013, October 10, 2013, p. 81.

[10]   Congressional-Executive Commission on China, Annual Report 2013, October 10, 2013, p. 81.

[11]   Congressional-Executive Commission on China, Annual Report 2013, October 10, 2013, p. 79; Flora Sapio, "Shuanggui and Extralegal Detention in China," China Information 22:7 (2008); and Andrew Jacobs, "Accused Chinese Party Members Face Harsh Discipline," New York Times, June 14, 2012. http://www.nytimes.com/2012/06/15/world /asia/accused-chinese-party-members-face-harsh-discipline.html.

[12]   Congressional-Executive Commission on China, Annual Report 2013, October 10, 2013, p. 79.

[13]   Human Rights Watch, "'An Alleyway in Hell': China's Abusive 'Black Jails'," November 2009, http://www.hrw.org/sites/default/files/reports /china1109web_1.pdf; and Phelim Kine, "Beijing's Black Jails," Foreign Policy,   March   15,   2012.   http://blog.foreignpolicy.com/posts /2012/03/15/beijings_black_jails.

[14]   Sharon LaFraniere and Dan Levin, "Assertive Chinese Held in Metal Wards," New York Times, November 11, 2010. http://www.nytimes.

com/2010/11/12/world/asia/12psych.html?pagewanted=all&_r=0; Calum McLeod, "Chinese Citizens Sent to Mental Hospitals to Quiet Dissent," USA Today, December 29, 2011. http://usatoday30.usatoday. com/news/world/story/2011-12-28/china-mental-hospitals/52260592/1; and Robin Munro, "The Ankang: China's Special Psychiatric Hospitals," Journal of Comparative Law 1:1 (2006).

[15] U.S. Department of State, Bureau of Democracy, Human Rights and Labor, "China (includes Tibet, Hong Kong, and Macau)," Country Reports on Human Rights Practices for 2013. http://www.state.gov /documents/organization/220402.pdf.

[16] Laogai Research Foundation, Laogai Handbook 2007-2008, (Washington, DC, 2008), p.3.

[17] Congressional-Executive Commission on China, Hearing on Working Conditions and Worker Rights in China: Recent Developments, testimony of Harry Wu, July 31, 2012.

[18] Ren Ke, "Commentary: Reform of Labor Re-education System Inevitable," Xinhua (English edition), October 11, 2012. http://news.xinhuanet.com/english/indepth/2012-10/11/c_131900685.htm.

[19] Thomas Lum, "Human Rights in China and U.S. Policy," Congressional Research Service, June 19, 2013. https://www.fas.org/sgp /crs/row/R43000.pdf.

[20] Sanne Deckwitz, Gulag vs. Laogai: The Function of Forced Labour Camps in the Soviet Union and China, (Utrecht University, January 2012), p. 45.

[21] Sanne Deckwitz, Gulag vs. Laogai: The Function of Forced Labour Camps in the Soviet Union and China (Utrecht University, January 2012), p. 45; and Laogai Research Foundation, Laogai Handbook 2007-2008, (Washington, DC, 2008), p.156.

[22] Sanne Deckwitz, Gulag vs. Laogai: The Function of Forced Labour Camps in the Soviet Union and China (Utrecht University, January 2012), p. 45.

[23] Nicole Kempton and Nan Richardson eds., Laogai: The Machinery of Repression in China (Brooklyn, NY: Umbrage Editions, 2009), p. 68.

[24] U.S. Department of State, Trafficking in Persons Report 2012: Country Narratives: A-C (June 2012), p. 118.

[25] Thomas Lum, "Human Rights in China and U.S. Policy," Congressional Research Service, July 18, 2011. http://www.fas.org/sgp/crs/row /RL34729.pdf.

[26] Congressional Executive Commission on China, Annual Report 2013, October 10, 2013, p. 90.

[27] Shohret Hoshur and Joshua Lipes, "Farmers Sent to Reeducation Camp," Radio Free Asia, August 15, 2011. http://www.rfa.org /english/news/uyghur/farmers-08152011181847.html; and Guru Choegyi and Lobsang Sherab, "Four Tibetan Monks Released from Labor Camp," Radio Free Asia, August 13, 2013. http://www.rfa.org/english /news/tibet/released-08132013165448.html.

[28] U.S. Department of State, Trafficking in Persons Report 2012: Country Narratives: A-C, June 2012, p. 118.

[29] 22 U.S.C. § 7002, as amended by Section 635 of Public Law 109-108.

[30] U.S.-China Economic and Security Review Commission, 2008 Annual Report to Congress, November 2008, p. 330.

[31] U.S.-China Economic and Security Review Commission, 2008 Annual Report to Congress, November 2008, p. 321.

[32] U.S. Department of Labor, List of Goods Produced by Child Labor or Forced Labor. http://www.dol.gov/ilab/programs/OCFT/2013TVPRA_ Infographic.pdf.

[33] Chinese Human Rights Defenders, "Re-education through Labor Abuses Continue Unabated: Overhaul Long Overdue," February 4, 2009, p. 32-33. http://docs.law.gwu.edu/facweb/dclarke/public/CHRD_RTL_Report. pdf; Laogai Research Foundation, Laogai Handbook 2007-2008, (Washington, DC, 2008), p.306; and "Jilin Prov. Women's Prison Packing and Color Printing Plant." Translation by Authors. http://idc.dg328.com/jilin_company_69900.html.

[34] Paul Danahar, "Coke Says No China Jail Labour," BBC News, May 21, 2007. http://news.bbc.co.uk/2/hi/asiapacific/6675343.stm; and Sky News, "The Real Thing: Forced Labour Linked to Coke," February 27, 2008. http://news.sky.com/story/572691/the-real-thing-forced-labour-linked-to-coke.

[35] Coca Cola Corporation, "Transparency in Supply Chains: Addressing Forced Labor & Human Trafficking," 2013. http://www.coca-colacompany.com/our-company/transparency-in-supply-chains-addressing-forced-labor-humantrafficking.

[36] Laogai Research Foundation, "Not for Sale: Advertising Forced Labor Products for Illegal Export," February 2010. http://www.laogai.org/sites /default/files/laogai_ads_report020410.pdf; and Global Manufacturer Pages, "Yunnan Jinma Mining Machinery Works,"

http://www.mfgpages.com/company/Yunnan-Jinma-Mining-Machinery-4628389.

[37] Lisa Murray and Angus Grigg, "Qantas in China Prison Labour Row," *Australian Financial Review*, June 26, 2013. http://www.afr.com/p/business/companies/qantas_in_china_prison_labour_row_yn60kkiVeQo yy4DzD3VrWP.

[38] Electrolux, "Regarding alleged Prison Labor in China," May 29, 2013. http://group.electrolux.com/en/regarding-alleged-prison-labor-in-china/.

[39] Behind Lies 09, "Products Made with Slave Labor at the Hebei Province Women's Forced Labor Camp," July 12, 2012. http://behindlies09.wordpress.com/2012/07/12/products-made-with-slave-labor-at-the-hebei-provincewomens-forced-labor-camp-photos/.

[40] Minghui.org, "Atrocities Behind the Products Made by Slave Labor in Inner Mongolia Women's Prison," March 17, 2012. http://www.en.minghui.org/html/articles/2012/3/17/132139.html.

[41] Serena Solomon, "Plea for Help From Man Claiming to Be Chinese Prisoner Found in Saks Bag," DNAinfo New York, April 29, 2014. http://www.dnainfo.com/new-york/20140429/midtown/plea-for-help-from-man-claiming-bechinese-prisoner-found-saks-bag.

[42] Yang Chen, "Detained American Provides Glimpse Into Chinese Forced Labor Practices," Voice of America, April 24, 2014. http://www.voanews.com/content/detained-american-provides-glimpse-into-chinese-forcedlabor-practices/1900718.html; Yang Chen and Chang Xiao, "An American scholar's experience imprisoned in China" Democratic China (Chinese edition), April 16, 2014. Translation by Authors. http://minzhuzhongguo.org/ArtShow.aspx?AID=39748.

[43] Danny Vincent, "China Used Prisoners in Lucrative Internet Gaming Work," The Guardian, May 25, 2011. http://www.guardian.co.uk/world/2011/may/25/china-prisoners-internet-gaming-scam?CMP=twt_gu; Herald Sun, "Chinese Labour Camp Prisoners Forced to Play World of Warcraft in Gold Farming Racket, Says Detainee," May 26, 2011. http://www.heraldsun.com.au/news/victoria/chinese-labour-prisoners-world-of-warcraft-jixi-re-education-camp-scam/story-e6frf7lf-1226063434889; and Uri Friedman, "Video Game 'Gold Farming' and Chinese Prison Labor," Atlantic Wire, May 26, 2011. http://www.theatlanticwire.com/global/2011/05/video-game-gold-farming-chinese-prison-labor/38178/.

[44] Danny Vincent, "China Used Prisoners in Lucrative Internet Gaming Work," Guardian, May 25, 2011. http://www.guardian.co.uk/world /2011/may/25/china-prisoners-internet-gaming-scam?CMP=twt_gu.

[45] Danny Vincent, "China Used Prisoners in Lucrative Internet Gaming Work," Guardian, May 25, 2011. http://www.guardian.co.uk /world/2011/may/25/china-prisoners-internet-gaming-scam?CMP=twt_gu.

[46] Andrew Jacobs, "Behind Cry for Help from China Labor Camp," New York Times, June 11, 2013. http://www.nytimes.com/2013/06 /12/world/asia/man-details-risks-in-exposing-chinas-forced-labor.html.

[47] Lens Magazine (Chinese edition), "Walking Out of Masanjia," April 2013. Translation by Authors.

[48] Du Bin (Director), "Above the Ghosts' Heads: The Women of Masanjia Labour Camp," [Video file], (2013). Translation by Authors. http://acopy.net/en/content/above-ghosts%E2%80%99-heads-women-masanjia-labor-camp.

[49] Lens Magazine (Chinese edition), "Walking Out of Masanjia," April 2013. Translation by Authors; and Du Bin (Director), "Above the Ghosts' Heads: The Women of Masanjia Labour Camp," [Video file], (2013). Translation by Authors. http://acopy.net/en/content/above-ghosts%E2%80%99-heads-women-masanjia-labor-camp.

[50] Qiao Long and Hai Nan, "China Hits Back at Magazine Over Labor Camp Expose," Radio Free Asia, May 6, 2013. http://www.rfa.org/english/news/china/expose-05062013151906.html.

[51] Fung Yat-Yiu and Qiao Long, "Masanjia Filmmaker Held in Beijing over 'Illegal Publishing'," Radio Free Asia, June 11, 2013. http://www.rfa.org/english/news/china/du-bin-06112013134904.html.

[52] Xinhua (Chinese edition), "Liaoning Investigation Group: The Article 'Walking Out of Masanjia' Contains Serious Errors," April 19, 2013. http://news.xinhuanet.com/politics/2013-04/19/c_115460561.htm. Translation by Authors.

[53] Fung Yat-Yiu and Qiao Long, "Masanjia Filmmaker Held in Beijing Over 'Illegal Publishing'," Radio Free Asia, June 11, 2013, http://www.rfa.org/english/news/china/du-bin-06112013134904.html; and Amnesty International, "China Detains Photographer Who Exposed Labour Camp Abuses," June 14, 2013. http://www.amnesty.org /en/news/china-detains-photographer-who-exposed-labour-camp-abuses-2013-06-14.

[54] George Tsogas, Labor Regulation in a Global Economy (Armonk, NY: M.E. Sharpe, 2001), p. 92.

[55] Nicole Kempton and Nan Richardson, eds., Laogai: The Machinery of Repression in China (Brooklyn, NY: Umbrage Editions, 2009), p. 69.

[56] U.S. Immigration and Customs Enforcement National Intellectual Property Rights Coordination Center, Fact Sheet on Commercial Fraud Enforcement.   http://www.ice.gov/doclib/news/library/factsheets/pdf /commercialfraud.pdf.

[57] Discussion between U.S. Immigration and Customs Enforcement personnel and Commission staff, June 6, 2012.

[58] U.S. Immigration and Customs Enforcement, Office of International Affairs, "HSI OIA Attache' Beijing and IPRC Response to Questions from U.S.-China Economic and Security Review Commission on Prison Labor," letter to Commission staff, April 2013.

[59] U.S.-China Economic and Security Review Commission, Hearing on the Memoranda of Understanding Between the United States and China Regarding Prison Labor Products, testimony of James Ink, June 19, 2008, p. 39.   http://origin.www.uscc.gov/sites/default/files/transcripts /6.19.08HearingTranscript.pdf.

[60] U.S.-China Economic and Security Review Commission, 2008 Annual Report to Congress, November 2008, pp. 325-327.

[61] U.S. Immigration and Customs Enforcement, Office of International Affairs, "HSI OIA Attache' Beijing and IPRC Response to Questions from U.S.-China Economic and Security Review Commission on Prison Labor," letter to Commission staff, April 2013.

[62] U.S.-China Economic and Security Review Commission, 2008 Annual Report to Congress, November 2008, pp. 327-330.

[63] AMEMBASSY Beijing diplomatic cable, "Shandong Prison Labor Visit," July 27, 2009 (Message DTG 270952Z JUL 09, UNCLASSIFIED).

[64] U.S.-China Economic and Security Review Commission, 2008 Annual Report to Congress, November 2008, p. 328.

[65] 6U.S. Immigration and Customs Enforcement official (U.S. Department of Homeland Security), email interview with Commission staff, July 4, 2014.

[66] U.S.-China Economic and Security Review Commission, Hearing on the Memoranda of Understanding Between the United States and China Regarding Prison Labor Products, testimony of Daniel Ellis, June 19,

2008, p. 11. http://origin.www.uscc.gov/sites/default/files/transcripts /6.19.08HearingTranscript.pdf.

[67] U.S. Immigration and Customs Enforcement, Office of International Affairs, "HSI OIA Attache' Beijing and IPRC Response to Questions from U.S.-China Economic and Security Review Commission on Prison Labor," letter to Commission staff, April 2013.

[68] U.S. Senate Committee on Foreign Relations, Hearing on the U.S. Implementation of Prison Labor Agreements with China, testimony of Jeffrey Bader, May 21, 1997, p. 19. http://www.gpo.gov/fdsys/pkg /CHRG105shrg47725/pdf/CHRG-105shrg47725.pdf.

[69] Xinhua (English edition), "China to Abolish Reeducation Through Labor," November 15, 2013. http://news.xinhuanet.com/english /china/2013-11/15/c_132891921.htm.

[70] Ma Li, "Beijing RTL Bureau changed to the Education Correction Bureau under the auspices of the Ministry of Justice," Beijing News (Chinese edition), May 7, 2014. Translation by Authors. http://news163.com/14/0507/02/9RK0TATQ00014AEE.html.

[71] Ren Ke, "Commentary: Reform of Labor Re-education System Inevitable," Xinhua (English edition), October 11, 2012. http://news.xinhuanet.com/english/indepth/2012-10/11/c_131900685.htm.

[72] Zhao Xu, "Doors Slam Shut on 'Re-education' System," China Daily, December 11, 2013. http://usa.chinadaily.com.cn/china/2013-12/11/content_17166010.htm.

[73] Xinhua (English edition), "China to Abolish Reeducation Through Labor," November 15, 2013. http://news.xinhuanet.com/english/china /2013-11/15/c_132891921.htm; and Zhao Yinan, "Home/China/Society Man freed after posting 'improper information'," China Daily (English edition), November 21, 2012, http://www.chinadaily.com.cn/china/2012-11/21/content_15946282.htm.

[74] Stanley Lubman, "Bo Xilai's Gift to Chongqing: A Legal Mess," Wall Street Journal, April 12, 2012. http://blogs.wsj.com/chinarealtime /2012/04/12/bo-xilais-gift-to-chongqing-a-legal-mess/; Kathrin Hille, "Chongqing in limbo after Bo Xilai downfall," Financial Times, March 29, 2012. http://www.ft.com/intl/cms/s/0/08e64140-7960-11e1-b87e-00144feab49a.html?siteedition=intl#axzz1rheb2l9n; and Lilian Lin, "Time for Re-Education? Critics Take on China Labor Camp System," Wall Street Journal, August 16, 2012.

http://blogs.wsj.com/chinarealtime/2012/08/16/time-for-re-education-critics-take-on-china-labor-campsystem/.

[75] Malcolm Moore, "China abolishes its labour camps and releases prisoners," Telegraph, January 9, 2014. http://www.telegraph.co.uk /news/worldnews/asia/china/10561434/China-abolishes-its-labour-camps-and-releasesprisoners.html; and John Ruwitch, "A Jail By Another Name: China Labor Camps Now Drug Detox Centers," Reuters, December 2, 2013. http://www.reuters.com /article/2013/12/02/us-china-campsidUSBRE9B10CQ20131202.

[76] Human Rights Watch, "China: End Re-Education Through Labor Without Loopholes," November 15, 2013. http://www.hrw.org/news/2013/11/15/china-end-re-education-through-labor-without-loopholes. Chen Qun, "Demolition of the Re-education Through Labor System Is a Progress in China's Rule of Law," China-US Focus, December 9, 2013. http://www.chinausfocus.com/political-social-development/demolition-of-the-reeducationthrough-labor-system-is-a-progress-in-chinas-rule-of-law/; and Zhou Zunyou, "Abolition of Re-education Through Labor a Milestone," China Daily (U.S. edition), December 5, 2013. http://usa.chinadaily.com.cn/epaper/2013- 12/05 /content_17153920.htm.

[77] Dui Hua Foundation, "RTL: Reporters Shed Some Light on Reform Projects," December 11, 2012. http://www.duihuahrjournal.org /2012/12/rtl-reporters-shed-some-light-on-reform.html; and Zhou Zunyou, "Abolition of Re-education Through Labor a Milestone," China Daily (U.S. edition), December 5, 2013. http://usa.chinadaily.com.cn /epaper/2013-12/05/content_17153920.htm.

[78] John Ruwitch, "A Jail By Another Name: China Labor Camps Now Drug Detox Centers," Reuters, December 2, 2013. http://www.reuters.com/article/2013/12/02/us-china-camps-idUSBRE9B10CQ20131202; Xinhua (English edition), "China to Abolish Reeducation Through Labor," November 15, 2013. http://news.xinhuanet.com/english/china/2013-11/15/c_132891921.htm; and Zhou Zunyou, "Abolition of Reeducation Through Labor a Milestone," China Daily (U.S. edition), December 5, 2013. http://usa.chinadaily.com.cn/epaper/2013-12/05/content_17153920.htm; Ma Li, "Beijing RTL Bureau changed to the Education Correction Bureau under the auspices of the Ministry of Justice," Beijing News (Chinese edition), May 7, 2014. Translation by Authors. http://news163.com/14/0507/02/9RK0TATQ00014AEE.html.

[79] Open Source Center, Reported PRC Civil Disturbances in 2013, April 11, 2014. ID: CHR2014041132236657

[80] Tariff Act of 1930, 19 U.S. Code 19 § 1307, "Convict-Made Goods; Importation   Prohibited."   http://www.law.cornell.edu/uscode/text/19/1307.

[81] Tariff Act of 1930, 19 U.S. Code 19 § 1307, "Convict-Made Goods; Importation   Prohibited."   http://www.law.cornell.edu/uscode/text/19/1307.

[82] 18 U.S. Code Section 1761, "Transportation or Importation." http://www.law.cornell.edu/uscode/text/18/1761.

[83] Jamie Strawbridge, "Business Groups Wary of Labor Provisions in Finance Customs Bill," Inside U.S. Trade, November 6, 2009. http://www.laborrights.org/stop-child-forced-labor/news/12218.

[84] Library of Congress Thomas Database, "Bill Summary & Status – S.1631 All Congressional Actions." http://thomas.loc.gov/cgi-bin/bdquery/z?d111:SN01631:@@@X.

INDEX

H

I

Q

R

X